So, You're New to Sales

Printed in the United States of America

FIRST EDITION

Library of Congress Cataloging-in-Publication Data
        Flanagan, Bryan
        So, You're New To Sales / Flanagan, Bryan

        ISBN-10 0983156506
        ISBN-13 9780983156505

Business   2. Sales I. Title

DEDICATION

I am successful because I followed the number one rule of success: marry well!

Thank you, Cyndi.

Parents don't produce better children. Children produce better parents.

Thank you, Patrick and Quinn.

TABLE OF CONTENTS

Acknowledgements

Every sales professional risks hearing "no" at each point of contact with prospects. These men and women are truly champions in their organizations. They are in the marketplace competing every day. Each understands the pressure, the stress, the stigma, the loneliness, and the risks of the sales profession. Each also understands the rewards, the exhilaration, and the thrill of sales success! Thanks to all the sales professionals who positively impacted my career and my life.

The book you are holding passed through numerous hands before it was ready for yours.

Thanks to Zig Ziglar for believing in me enough to trust me with his clients, his philosophy, and his reputation. Thanks to Jean Abernathy Ziglar who puts up with my sense of humor.

Thanks to our Ziglar team who encouraged me along the way.

Bert Newman for your patience with my "technology" challenges.

Jill Tibbels for encouraging me to trust my instincts about my sales philosophy.

Kayla Mitchell for your patience with my "attention to detail" challenges.

Katherine Lemons for holding me accountable to deadlines. (I hate deadlines!)

Margaret Garrett, Michael McGowan, and Joe Eaves for reinforcing the selling principles we teach.

Cindy Oates for her smiles and encouraging pep talks.

Julie Ziglar Norman for her insights, direction, and professional advice.

Tom Ziglar for the leadership vision that continues to move me forward.

Laurie Magers for 26 years of guidance and friendship.

Foreword

Anyone who has known me for any amount of time knows that I believe it is absolutely essential to not only tell people what they need and want to know, but to also give them the tools and instruction they need to accomplish their objectives. If you're just getting started in the career that paved the way to my success, my friend and associate of 26 years, Bryan Flanagan, has written exactly what you need to read in his powerful, succinct, no-fluff, all-good-stuff, book *So, You're New to Sales*.

Bryan Flanagan is one of the most inspiring, encouraging good-finders I have ever known. Bryan's great sense of humor, his strong faith, his commitment to his family and to being the best he can be in his chosen profession, have earned him my respect, admiration and love. I am grateful that he is a loyal member of the Ziglar team and that his powerful skill set has been so instrumental in helping our sales training be recognized as the best in the world. His vision is clear and precise and in true leadership style, he is a role model by example. He is not only an outstanding speaker, his success in sales and his success in teaching others how to sell have kept him in great demand throughout his career.

Bryan's book gives you word for word examples of how to sell from hello to goodbye. Learning his powerful process for selling will save you countless hours of making unfruitful sales calls and increase your bottom line in a much shorter period of time. The advantages of starting your sales career with the most succinct, concise sales book I've ever read are countless! Start reading *So, You're New to Sales* right now and have your pen and notebook handy. Bryan is about to teach you how to become a professional salesperson by teaching you how to communicate the benefits, values and advantages of the product or service you are selling. I often say nothing happens until somebody sells somebody something – so, get to it! Go sell somebody something!

Zig Ziglar

Introduction

Welcome to the world of professional selling. You are in for the ride of your life. Why? Because of all the "helping professions" in this world, professional selling ranks with the best of them.

Selling is an honorable profession. Sales professionals are held to a higher standard than other professionals. Why? Because salespeople are trained in the skills of persuading and influencing. Therefore, we must hold ourselves to the highest ethical standards.

Much like any other profession, success in sales requires dedication, commitment, and a strong desire to excel. At Ziglar, Inc., we emphasize three components to overall success: *the will, the skill, and the refill*. The purpose of this book is:

- To teach you how to sell. That's right. It is just that simple and straightforward. The purpose of this book is to teach you the practical skills, techniques, and strategies necessary for sales success. We refer to this as your *skill*.

- To prepare you for the emotional aspect of sales success. Your attitude is an essential element in successful selling. Whether you are a rookie or a veteran salesperson, your attitude is vital to your success. We refer to this as your *will*.

To encourage you to continue to learn your profession. I have been in sales for more than 40 years and I have never known anyone who has ever "graduated" from learning to sell. You should continue to invest in your *skill* and *will* with new information to support your success. We refer to this as your *refill.*

Here's a key point: If you apply the lessons in this book you will be prepared to make an effective sales call. You will fully understand the skills necessary to make a sales call with confidence and competency.

The bottom line is this. You will learn how to sell, how to prospect, how to initiate contact with a prospect, how to make an effective prospect-centered sales call, how to "lead with need" when presenting your solution, how to manage resistance/objections, how to gain agreement, and how to conduct yourself in a professional manner. Along the way, we'll talk about the mistakes to avoid and how to handle the emotional demands of the profession.

Selling can be a most rewarding career for you if you desire to:

- help people
- solve problems
- create opportunities for people who didn't think those possibilities applied to them
- assist people to better their lives
- help others achieve their dreams
- contribute to the profits of businesses and organizations
- meet a variety of people
- be a teammate
- create positive atmospheres

- challenge yourself to grow and develop
- provide for yourself and your family
- be rewarded for your efforts
- be recognized
- earn a living
- compete on a daily basis

Well, you get the picture. It is a great profession. It is an honorable profession. What you do as a sales professional *counts*. What you do *matters*. Respect what you do; embrace the profession that you've chosen, or the one that has chosen you.

CHAPTER 1:

The Psychology of Sales

Selling Didn't Come Naturally for Me

I am not a *natural-born* salesperson. Perhaps you aren't either. Here's the good news: there is hope for both of us! I am confident that if you have the **will** to learn to succeed in the world of professional selling, you can acquire the **skill** to succeed in the world of professional selling. That's the purpose of this book you have in your hands: to help you reach sales success.

I had to learn to be an effective sales professional. It has been hard work to learn my profession. And, I am so glad I did learn, because selling has been very rewarding to me and my family. Selling has allowed me to provide for my loved ones. Selling has allowed me to enroll my children in the university of their choice versus where I could afford to send them. Selling has literally taken me around the world. I honor the sales profession. I respect the sales profession.

However, as stated earlier, I am not a natural-born salesperson. I am jealous of those natural-born salespeople who caught on easily and didn't struggle with the stigma of being one of those "sales types." Looking back, I wouldn't trade places with the natural-born salesperson. I am glad I had my doubts, uncertainties, and fears. (By the way, those are called DUFs. This book will teach you how to confront and overcome the DUFs.) These have made me more effective, more confident, more competent, and more successful.

There is hope for the novice salesperson. There is hope for the salesperson who is struggling with moving to the next sales plateau. There is hope for the veteran sales professional who needs to be reminded what is necessary to remain a top producer. There is hope for the "non-traditional" salesperson; the person who has been mandated to sell. There is hope for the professional who doesn't want to be a professional salesperson but must be a professional who can sell! Yes, if you have the will to succeed, there is hope for you to develop the skill to succeed.

This book provides the guidelines to do just that. If you implement the principles outlined in *So, You're New To Sales* you will be able to:

- Succeed in sales
- Assist buyers in solving problems and enhancing their current situation
- Take pride in your profession
- Gain confidence as a sales professional
- Understand the psychology of selling
- Conduct effective sales calls
- Implement a prospect-centered sales process
- Initiate contacting prospective clients
- Manage sales resistance and sales objections

- Handle the emotional demands of the sales profession
- Reach your professional goals
- Enjoy the world of professional selling!!!

To receive the best return on your investment, the following strategies are suggested:

1. Convert this book to your actual day-to-day sales environment. That is, modify the concepts/techniques into your real-world sales situations. By that I mean an example may refer to a tangible product such as automobiles, homes, computers, cell phones. Yet, you may sell an intangible (i.e., professional services, advice, insurance, warranty, protection...). You will have to use your industry knowledge to adjust the technique to your situation.

2. Try the technique more than once! To do something well you must first do it poorly. On your first few attempts, you will not be comfortable nor will you be confident with the sales skill or technique. Give yourself a chance to be successful by implementing the technique several times. You just might find that you are effective before you become comfortable!

3. Ask for advice. Ask senior sales professionals for insights into effective selling techniques. I love sales because it is such an individual activity. If I put forth a consistently effective effort, I will be consistently rewarded. Yet, I have never been successful in a vacuum. I have a team that I rely on to contribute to my success. Don't hesitate to ask for help.

4. Contact me. My email is <u>bflanagan@ziglar.com</u>. I am open to assisting you in any way I can to better your understanding and use of the principles outlined in this book.

The book is organized in easy-to-read and easy-to-apply lessons. Each lesson is designed to be brief and to the point so that you can read a section, put the book down, and go sell somebody something!

I look forward to contributing to your growth as a top producing sales professional!!!

Now, let's get started...

Are You Also an *Accidental* Salesperson?

I am an accidental salesperson. When I was in college, I wanted to be a high school basketball coach. All my fraternity brothers urged me to major in marketing. They told me, "You have a sales personality. You should be in sales. That's a perfect fit for you." Those words frightened me. I didn't know a thing about selling. Besides, my mother raised me the way your mother raised you. She told me, "Never talk to strangers and don't ask people for money!" (Sound familiar?) So, what did I do? I became a salesman! Talking to strangers and asking people for money is how I earn a living!

During my second senior year at Louisiana State University (I graduated in the half of the class that made the top half possible) Cyndi and I had been dating for four years and were planning to wed. But I had no job and Cyndi was spending her final semester as a student teacher. In an effort to find employment, I answered an ad in the Student Aid office for part-time work with the IBM Corporation. I was fortunate that I dressed properly for the first interview in my life. I actually wore a three-piece suit...and all three pieces matched! Again, I was lucky because I was hired despite having no experience in sales, business, or the marketplace.

I began working as a delivery boy for the IBM Corporation in Baton Rouge, Louisiana. This is how old I am: my first job was delivering typewriters for the Office Products Division of IBM. The division sold and serviced electric typewriters and copying machines. Yes, for you young readers, before "keyboarding" there was "typing." My year-long, part-time job allowed us to get married, to live in married student housing, and to finish our degrees. Once I graduated, IBM hired me as a full-time sales representative.

My 90-day training consisted of two months in the branch office and one month in downtown Dallas at the National Training Center. In those days, we estimated that the company invested roughly $50,000 in preparing the salesperson to enter a sales territory. Once my training concluded, I was assigned my first sales territory. I was given six parishes (other states refer to these as counties) outside of Baton Rouge, Louisiana. But I had a problem: I could not sell! After investing $50,000 on my training, IBM had a salesperson who couldn't sell. It was not IBM's fault. I learned long ago that I am responsible for my success. I respect IBM and certainly am honored to have been a part of Big Blue for 14 years. (I still have my white shirts and 12-pound wing-tipped shoes!) I experienced a very difficult year my first year in sales. Now, that doesn't mean I didn't sell a lot. I did sell a lot: I sold my furniture, I sold my car, I sold some of my stocks…. If you have been in sales for a while, you will know it wasn't entirely my fault. You see, they gave me a bad territory! My prospects were strange. Some of them would actually sit around the coffee table in their offices reading the obituary column in the newspaper trying to figure out why people died in alphabetical order!

Can You Identify?

I struggled a great deal trying to become a salesperson, but I never pulled it all together. I battled the stigma of being a salesman. I had no confidence in my selling skills. I didn't know how to conduct a sales interview and I was at a loss when a prospect said my price was too high. When a prospect said he was happy with the current equipment, I would turn and almost sprint to my car. I was unsure how to pick up the telephone and set appointments and I took "no" personally. When I got into a selling slump, I stayed in that slump for a long time. I couldn't handle the emotional demands of selling. I became an inactive salesperson. I jokingly say that I "aggressively waited for my phone to ring." I was inconsistent in achieving my sales quota. I was miserable.

My mother and father had instilled in their three children a strong work ethic. I knew that I had to tough it out. I decided to get serious about my success. I began to learn things. I learned *timid salespeople have skinny kids*! That converted me from passive to a bit more assertive. I started to do things better. I invested in myself by joining a local Toastmasters International Club. I began to gain confidence in my abilities to speak, communicate, and present. Inwardly, I had low self-esteem. Because of my desire to help train new salespeople at our local branch office, IBM promoted me to the National Training Center in Dallas, Texas, as a sales instructor. (Those who can, do; those who can't, teach; and those who can't teach, teach sales!!!)

I was now at the national center competing with twenty-four other staff members for future sales management positions. I had no confidence in myself as a professional or as a person. I thought of myself as a little guy from a little town with a little image of myself. I was competing with men and women from large cities:

Cathy was from Chicago, Linda was from New York, Roger from Boston, Ron from Seattle. I didn't think I could compete with them. As mentioned, my self-esteem or "deserve level" was low.

Someone noticed my struggle and suggested I invest in a book by a man named Zig Ziglar. The book was entitled *See You at the Top* and it cost $12.95. At the time, I was not a book-worm nor was I a tape-worm. I was not reading books nor was I listening to audio cassettes. I was not involved with Toastmasters at the time and I was not investing in myself. However, when I got to page 48 of Zig's book, my life changed. One sentence in that book forever changed my personal life as well as my professional life. That one sentence read, "You cannot consistently perform in a manner that is inconsistent with the way you see yourself."

My wife had told me similar things for the eight years we'd been married. But until I read those words, I was missing success by a distance of 12 inches. That's the distance from my head to my heart. For $50,000, IBM had taught me the intellectual side, the head side of selling. For $12.95 Zig Ziglar taught me the heart side of selling, the belief side of selling. Don't get me wrong, you need both. However, I was missing the heart side. I discovered that I had been in sales for six years, but selling wasn't in me. I think other salespeople experience the same feeling at times.

You see, I was trying to give away something I did not possess. That is, I was trying to transfer to my customers something I didn't possess: confidence in myself and in my ability to help solve a problem. I did not possess confidence in myself and because of that I had no confidence in communicating how I could help someone solve his or her challenges. I believed it with my head but not with my heart. That's why both the **will** and the **skill** are so vital for new salespeople.

This discovery made a HUGE difference. I felt better about myself, I felt better about the profession of sales. I truly believed that I deserved to be successful. I truly believed that I could add value to a person's business. I truly believed that I could positively impact the bottom line and increase productivity. Yes, I was missing sales success by 12 inches, the distance from my head to my heart. Once I completed that short distance I began to produce great sales results. If you are struggling with a similar issue, my desire is that you will also get serious about investing in your "deserve level." You *deserve* to be successful. You *deserve* to professionally represent your company and yourself in solving problems that your prospects experience. You *deserve* to be rewarded when you are successful in helping solve those problems.

Two Elements Helped

There were two elements that contributed to my becoming an effective salesperson:

1. Learning my profession
2. Respecting my profession

Learning My Profession

You never graduate from selling. You are always growing. Successful salespeople invest in themselves by learning and studying their profession. There were a couple of things I learned from this. One, you should invest more in yourself than you do in your career. You should, no, you **must**, be a constant student. School is never out for the professional. Enroll in "Automobile University." By that I mean use your car as a learning chamber. Listen to audio recordings that will not only give you a motivational lift, but will prepare you for your sales day, for your next sales call, for your trip home to the family. The reason I encourage you to invest in yourself is this: **Personal growth precedes professional growth. Better people build better sales professionals.**

Respecting My Profession

Selling is an honorable profession because selling is something you do **with** the prospect, not **to** the prospect. If the sales transaction is not mutually benefitting you and the prospect, then cease your selling activities, ask for a referral, thank the prospect for his or her time, and conclude the interview.

Let me give you an example. I was training new luxury car salespeople over a period of several weeks. I noticed one young man who was still struggling with the title of "car salesman" and with the challenge of working on straight commission. During class I asked if he would role play with me on three questions. I asked him to think of a client whom he had sold a car four or five months earlier. When he said he had one in mind, I then asked three questions:

1. Does the person still drive the unit you sold him? The answer was yes.

2. Do you still have all the commission you made when you sold the car? The answer was no.

3. The last question: who got the best deal, you or the client? The answer was, of course, the client.

Because of the sales efforts of this young car salesman, the client will enjoy the value of the transaction for years to come. The car owner has a long-term benefit. The salesman has a benefit, but it is not as long-term.

I have the same question for you: when you sell your product or service, who gets the best deal? The answer is the client (I'll help you with the difficult questions...).

Take pride in the fact that you can positively impact the lives of your prospects. If you are a commissioned salesperson, you never get paid until you've helped some other person (your prospect) improve his or her life in some fashion. Yes, selling is a great profession!

Likes and Dislikes

During my sales training workshops I often ask the participants, "What do you like about the sales profession and what do you dislike about the sales profession?" The answers are then listed on a flip chart in the front of the room.

These are the answers I often receive:

What I LIKE:	What I DISLIKE:
Freedom	Rejection
Working with people	Uncertainty
Solving problems	Pressure
Money	Stigma
Control my future	The ups and downs

I then ask, "What is the common denominator between the two lists?" You will notice as you review the lists, there is not one policy, procedure, or product on either side. So, what is the connection between the two?

Here it comes. Are you ready? The connection is how the salesperson handles the *emotional demands* of the sales profession.

That's right. How you handle the emotional side of selling. More so than any profession, sales professionals move on emotions.

Here is an example. Let's compare the accounting profession to that of sales. I admire accountants because I don't have an analytical bone in my body. I can't do what an accountant does. (Do you know what I do when my bank book doesn't balance? I change banks!) How long is the reporting period for an accountant? A month? A quarter? A year? How long is the reporting period for a salesperson? Every door knock, every handshake, every phone call. Our reporting periods come fast and furious. We are going to hear the word "no" more often than other professionals. We will have more opportunities to fail than other professionals. Therefore, we must be emotionally stronger than other professionals.

One of the many reasons I love selling is that success doesn't depend on the color of your skin. It does, however, depend on the thickness of your skin. When you became a salesperson, you accepted the chance of hearing "no."

Here is the key: you don't have to like everything about selling to be outrageously successful. That's right. You don't have to like every aspect of selling to succeed. I find that statement to be liberating. You don't have to like all the activities associated with selling. But you do have to perform them.

As you progress through your sales career, you have to continually evaluate yourself, your skills, your attitudes, and your growth. Do not fall into the trap of "beating yourself up." Salespeople are famous for holding themselves to unreachable standards. Yes, you need high standards. However, you need realistic standards. Give yourself permission to be successful. You have to stop being critical of yourself when you stop being fair to yourself. Do not unfairly criticize yourself. Loosen up! Relax! Remember, <u>angels fly</u> <u>because they take themselves lightly</u>.

Definitions

It will be helpful for you to familiarize yourself with the following terms used throughout the book.

> **Preparation and Planning**: Gathering information to assist you in contacting and calling on the prospect. This includes research, social networking, personal contact, and third party information. Proper planning gives you a competitive edge.
>
> **Prospecting**: Identifying the organizations and individuals that have a potential need for your products/services/solutions.
>
> **Product:** Interpreting how your products/services/solutions benefit your prospects and communicating that value to them.
>
> **Process:** Implementing a formula for focusing on the prospect's needs, issues, and concerns.
>
> **The Person:** Possessing the confidence in yourself and understanding your role as a sales professional.

16 Professional Selling Principles

Here are some principles you may want to think about during your sales day.

Principle #1: Selling is a *process*, not an event.

This is one of the essentials of successful selling. Selling is a step-by-step process involving the buyer and the seller. Selling is not one-sided. It is not a process for the salesperson only. It is a methodology of discovering what problem or concern the buyer has, then assisting in solving that problem or concern.

So, You're New to Sales introduces the Sales P.R.O.C.E.S.S. Formula of professional selling. This is a step-by-step methodology addressing the seven steps necessary to sell with confidence and competency. Whether you are selling a tangible product or an intangible service, the Sales P.R.O.C.E.S.S. will serve you well. The reason is that this process allows the salesperson to focus on the prospect and his or her needs, issues and concerns. You'll enjoy greater sales success when implementing this process.

The process is outlined below. You may be using a similar process. However, the seven-step process below forms the acrostic "PROCESS." Each of the steps is a link in the process that provides a methodology to move to the next step. By knowing where you are in the process, and knowing where the prospect is in the process, you have a better chance of successfully reaching a favorable conclusion.

STEP	PURPOSE	HOW
Prepare, Plan, and Prospect	Get ready! Establish your call objectives	Research, observe, be open to sales opportunities, initiate contact
Relate	Build trust/rapport	Focus on the prospect

Open a Dialogue to Uncover Needs	Determine N-I-C: Needs, Issues, and Concerns	Ask appropriate questions
Confirm Needs	Gain agreement that a need(s) exists	Upset prospect's "homeostatic balance"
Explain Your Recommendation	Introduce Solution	"Let me recommend . . ."
Sell the Value	Interpret the value of your solution	Communicate via the Prospect's Point of View
Simply Ask for the Objective	Reach Closure	AAFTO: Always Ask For the Objective

This book illustrates a specific sales process intended for those in the relationship sales environment. In other words, it works very effectively for environments conducive to establishing relationships, building long-term partnerships, and continuing to service and sell into existing accounts. At the same time, it provides an effective model for driving new business and replacing competitive installations.

Principle #2: <u>You make more money **solving problems** than you do by selling products!</u>

The only time a commissioned salesperson earns money is when he or she assists a prospect in improving his or her situation. It may be assisting the prospect in reducing stress, making or saving money, providing peace of mind, etc.

When you solve problems for prospects, you become a hero to them. You become a great resource to that person. To be a successful problem solver, you need to be others-focused. That is, you must pay attention to the other person's needs, issues, concerns, challenges. If you can identify those areas and then place the prospect in a position to solve them, the money will follow.

Principle #3: Prospects do things for their reasons, not your reasons!

As similar as prospects are, they also have major differences. Some people may purchase your solutions for monetary gain, others for prestige, and still others for the convenience and ease your solution offers. It is imperative you uncover the reason a person would exchange money for your product or service. In chapter six on "Open a Dialogue to Uncover Needs" you will learn to identify those reasons.

Principle #4: When selling yourself, you must believe in your product.

Your sales success depends on how you present yourself. Do your prospects see you as a poised, professional individual? Or, do they see you as a person who is uncomfortable and lacking confidence? Zig Ziglar claims that selling is nothing more than a transference of feeling. If you can transfer how you feel about your solution to the prospect, you'll have a customer for life.

The prospect buys you before buying your plan. You must first have that inner belief that you deserve to achieve the sale. Then you must believe that you can assist the prospect in improving his present situation. When you have that inner belief, that inner confidence, that belief you are worthy of success, your chances for success are greatly increased. This issue is addressed throughout *So, You're New to Sales*.

Principle #5: To be convincing to others, you must first be convinced yourself!

You can't give away something you don't possess. Therefore, you must be convinced your product or service is superior to the competition. No, I am not saying that you have to have the perfect solution. Perfect solutions usually don't exist. However, you must have a deep belief that your solution is the best fit for the prospect's needs.

Many years ago, I was selling a product I did not believe in. You guessed it, I did not sell it often. The product was dictation equipment. Since I didn't use dictation equipment for my correspondence, I didn't have a deep belief in the benefits of the product. Consequently, I did not sell it. However, once I began to use the equipment, I began to see the advantages it offered. It saved time and energy when I produced proposals and letters. I began to believe and I began to sell dictation equipment. You have to believe.

Principle #6: If it is to be, it is up to me.

Selling is a very personal activity. If you work hard you will be rewarded. If you do not work hard, you will not be rewarded.

Principle #7: Pressure selling is caused by a lack of prospects.

Prospects are the lifeblood of any sales organization. For new salespeople, prospects are the foundation on which to build a career. Most new salespeople don't receive a long list of existing clients. Therefore, it is important to always build your "prospect funnel." That is, create a list of potential buyers.

When you have a short list of prospects, you put pressure on those people to buy from you. That is not the reputation you want to create in the marketplace. If you have a short list of prospects, I don't want to be on that list. Why? Because you are going to call me all the time, you are going to push to meet with me. By always having a long list of prospects, you have more people to contact and you put less pressure on the ones on your list.

A key point about prospecting: you are always prospecting. You are not always selling, but you are always searching for potential buyers.

Principle #8: Your customers don't buy what you do; *they buy what you can do for them.*

This concept will be covered in "Sell the Value." In that chapter the strategy of selling values, advantages, and benefits is addressed. These have to be sold from the perspective of the prospect. Once you identify what the person wants, you can then present how your solutions meet those needs.

Principle #9: You can have everything in life you want, if you will just help enough other people get what they want!

Zig Ziglar built his entire career on this simple, yet powerful statement. Salespeople should embrace this philosophy. As a sales professional, you are trying to strengthen the prospect's position or environment or situation. If you can put a person in a position to reach his or her goals, you earn the prospect's trust and become a "trusted advisor."

Principle #10: Timid salespeople have skinny kids!

This is a humorous saying, the purpose of which is to have you smile or chuckle. However, there is a lot of truth in this sentence. It simply means if you aren't stepping up to the challenges, you aren't putting bread on the table. I will never suggest you be aggressive. I will tell you to be assertive in your sales activities, believe in yourself and your skills, and have certainty in your ability to solve prospects' problems.

It also means to be serious about your sales success. Be serious enough to ask questions of your company's sales leadership. Be serious enough to seek assistance when you need help.

Principle #11: You are only as good as your information.

Sales are not closed because you have a lot of facts. Sales are closed because you have a lot of information. The prospect may claim he has no money in the budget. That is a fact. However, if you understand why he is out of budget, perhaps you can better understand his concerns and place him in a position of avoiding budget problems in the future.

Principle #12: Whoever has the most information has the most influence.

Information is powerful. The more information you have, the better you can understand and relate to the prospect. The more information you have, the greater your chances of influencing the purchasing decision. In order to beat your competition, you don't have to be 10 times better than they are. You just have to have a bit more information than your competitor in order to push the decision to your side of the equation.

Principle #13: Prescription without diagnosis is malpractice in any profession.

This is the challenge for people new to sales. It is often more comfortable to talk about your products and services than it is to talk intelligently about the prospect's issues and concerns. Therefore, we are more comfortable talking about us than we are asking questions to find out about them. The key is this: **don't tell all you know until you know what to tell.**

You wouldn't trust a doctor who prescribed a treatment without identifying your pain and the source of your pain. Your prospects are the same way. They will not trust you unless you first perform some type of diagnosis. This is accomplished by asking questions, listening to the answers, and then connecting those answers to your solutions.

Principle #14: Process takes pressure off the person.

This is a huge principle for the new salesperson. Why? Because we often believe the personality is more important than the process. If I have the choice to tweak a process or a personality, I would rather tweak a process on a sales call than tweak a personality. You should put pressure on the process and take the pressure off of your personality.

Principle #15: Don't quote price until you've established value.

When you quote your price before you've communicated the values, advantages and benefits of your product or service, you will reduce your solution to a "commodity." This means you are just like every other competitor trying to win the prospect's business. If you've not established value, then no matter what price you quote, the prospect will believe it is too much money to spend for the return she is receiving for the money.

You should postpone talking price until you have established enough value in the prospect's mind to make a positive impact.

Principle #16: The intent behind your technique determines your ethics!

New salespeople are often concerned with "coming on too strong" with a prospect. I hear this all the time: "Oh, I couldn't use that question, I don't want to sound too sales-y!"

Let's say you have a product that enhances the prospect's current situation. In fact, you believe with all your heart that this solution is a good match for the prospect and you know by purchasing from you the prospect will greatly benefit. Now, let's say you do not ask that question because you are too uncomfortable to ask it. If that were the case, wouldn't you be doing the prospect a disservice, or an injustice?

If your intent behind asking a question is to help the prospect, then any question you ask is ethical.

On the other hand, if you are not sure this solution is the best for the prospect, you should cease your selling efforts until you know for sure this purchase will definitely contribute to his or her betterment.

The Four Stages of Growth

This next section is based on a model taken from Abraham Maslow's "Four Stages of Learning." Maslow's theory states that when learning a skill, we generally progress in four distinct stages. For our purposes, we will call these the "Four Stages of Sales Growth."

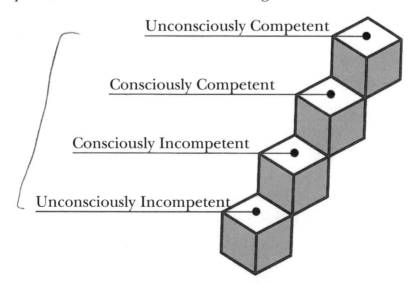

Unconsciously Competent

Consciously Competent

Consciously Incompetent

Unconsciously Incompetent

The first stage is where *you do not know you do not know*. This is called **Unconsciously Incompetent**. You may have found yourself in this stage when you were exposed to your company's products or services. You did not know the meaning of industry-specific terms or "buzz words." For example, later in the book you will be introduced to a sales concept called "upsetting the prospect's homeostatic balance." If you are not familiar with that term, or you have not heard it used in a sales context, you are at the first stage of growth: you don't know that you don't know.

The second stage is where *you know you do not know*. This is called **Consciously Incompetent.** You may be at this stage when you realize you aren't skilled in making phone calls in order to schedule appointments. Oh, you know how to use the telephone. However, you aren't proficient in communicating why a prospect should meet with you.

When you get to this stage, three things happen to you: first, your motivation disappears; second, your frustration rises; and third, you start to doubt yourself. You begin to have second thoughts about even being a sales professional. You talk to yourself by saying, "Oh, I should have stayed in customer service. Selling is a lot harder than anyone led me to believe!" This is the stage where you put pressure on yourself. Zig Ziglar says this is the stage where you develop "stinkin' thinkin'." You start to overly criticize yourself. Who is your worst critic? Of course, you are…unless you are married. (Just kidding: marriage is grand…divorce is four hundred grand!)

Two important points: First, it's okay to be at this stage, it is NOT okay to stay there. You need to progress through this stage. When you do, you will be more confident and feel better about yourself. Second, you need to know how to get out of this stage. Once again, my mentor, boss and friend Zig can help us out here.

Zig suggests you keep a *victory list* to remind you of your past successes. This *victory list* should include the things that gave you the most satisfaction and confidence. As you review your *victory list* you will be reminded that you have succeeded in the past and you are capable of succeeding in the future! You really should create a *victory list.*

The third stage of growth is the point where *you know you know.* This is called **Consciously Competent.** At this stage you can be productive. It is still not second nature to you, you are still not on "auto pilot," but you know what is required to succeed and you perform those tasks at a conscious level. After a while you will acquire the skills, techniques, and experiences to deliberately use the telephone to schedule sales appointments.

The fourth stage of growth is the stage where you are so good at something you reach the point *you don't know that you know.* This is called **Unconsciously Competent.** Now you are on "auto-pilot." Athletes call it "being in the zone." Oftentimes, new salespeople are in this stage in the area of building rapport and relationships with others. They are referred to as "people people." You know these types. They have never met a stranger. These are the people who talk on an elevator when they are the only ones on the elevator! They just take to people naturally and others are drawn to them. These salespeople couldn't tell you how they engage others in conversations; they just seem to have a knack for it.

Sometimes salespeople are referred to as "natural-born salespeople." If that's the case, they are usually in the Unconsciously Competent stage. They can produce activities and behaviors that lead to sales effectiveness. I am very jealous of that. The reason I am jealous is that I am NOT a natural-born salesman. It required a lot of trial and error on my part to be an effective salesman. In fact, if I rated my sales skills on Four Stages of Growth, I would accurately rank myself solidly in the Consciously Incompetent and Consciously Competent stages. For me, selling was an acquired skill. It was not a natural skill for me. I had to move up the steps in very small increments. However, I am glad I did because I think I am a better salesperson because of those incremental steps.

In my sales seminars I often tell the participants I am in the middle two stages of the growth chart. I also tell the participants that I am so excited about being at those stages because I still have plenty of room for growth and improvement. You see, after 40 years as a sales professional, **I am still growing**. My greatest victories as a salesperson are ahead of me. I am excited about that! You should be excited, also. Your future is ahead of you as well!

Let me use a sports analogy. Let's take my two boyhood heroes, Mickey Mantle and Ted Williams. Mickey Mantle is a Hall of Fame Baseball player. He hit 536 home runs and an additional 18 in World Series competition. He was a natural hitter. It was difficult for Mickey to move from Unconsciously Competent down to Consciously Competent. He was never a hitting instructor for the New York Yankees. You see, when he got into a sales slump, I mean, when he got into a batting slump, he couldn't move down to the Consciously Competent level and self-correct. No, when he experienced a batting slump he had to hit his way out of the slump. One of his biggest regrets was that he didn't end his career as a .300 hitter, one measure on which major league players are evaluated.

On the other hand, my other hero, Ted Williams, hit .344 as a lifetime batting average which is 46 points higher than Mickey's average. Williams hit 521 home runs, was the last player to hit over .400, and was arguably the greatest hitter in the history of the major leagues. Ted Williams was also Unconsciously Competent. However, Williams had the ability to move down to the third level to Consciously Competent. He could self-correct. His batting slumps were shorter in duration than Mickey's. Ted even wrote the book *The Science of Hitting.*

The challenge with natural-born salespeople is the same that natural-born athletes face: when things aren't going well, what do they do? Can the natural-born salesperson move down a level to Consciously Competent? Sometimes it is more difficult for them because they did not spend a lot of time in the Consciously Competent level when they were learning to sell.

So, if you aren't an Unconsciously Competent salesperson, there is hope. Yes, you too can grow into being an effective sales producer. Just continue to grow and invest in yourself.

Here is a mistake we make in sales departments. We often ask the superstar salesperson to coach the rookie salesperson. If the superstar is Unconsciously Competent and can't move back to the Consciously Competent level, this superstar will not be a very good coach. This only works if the rookie is a "clone" of the super-star. That is rarely the case. It is important for new salespeople to receive instruction from a coach who is Consciously Competent so that the coach can teach the skills the rookie needs to learn.

An important concept about the Four Stages of Growth: **you model from Stage Four (Unconsciously Competent) and you coach from Stage Three (Consciously Competent).**

The Four Stages of Growth Exercise

This exercise requires you to be very honest with yourself. No one else needs to see your answers. This is a three-part exercise.

1. Choose a selling skill that is needed for you to be successful.
2. Rate your proficiency in that skill on the growth chart. Are you at the second level, the third level...?

3. Provide evidence to support why you rated yourself at that stage.

Here's a personal example:

My skill is prospecting.

I rank myself at the third level, Consciously Competent.

The evidence: I attend networking organizations and provide 10-minute training topics. I gather the attendees' business cards and conduct a drawing by giving away Ziglar products. I then bring the business cards back to the office and distribute to the sales representatives.

I have met the three requirements: I chose a skill, prospecting. I rated myself at the third stage, Consciously Competent. I then provided specific evidence to support the ranking.

Your turn:

Skill:_____

Rate:_____

Evidence: _____

The following story illustrates the importance of this exercise. A few years ago I was called into a client's office to work with the new life insurance agents. As the participants were engaged in the exercise, I walked up to a young man named Troy. I asked what skill he chose. Here is the conversation that followed.

Troy: "Same as yours. I chose prospecting."

Bryan: "Where did you rank yourself?"

Troy: "Well, I rated myself as Consciously Incompetent. I'm not good at prospecting and I know I'm not good!"

Bryan: "Okay. What evidence do you have to support that ranking?"

Troy: "My manager has been harping on me to fill up my pipeline, fill up my pipeline. So, one afternoon last week, I came in and pounded the phone for an hour and set three appointments for this week."

Bryan: "Wait a minute. You said you weren't good at prospecting. But based on what you just said, and based on your evidence, you are good at prospecting. Why did you rate yourself so low?"

Troy: "Oh, I hate prospecting!"

I did not ask Troy if he liked prospecting. I asked Troy if he was any good at it. According to his evidence he was very good at it! He invested an hour and set three appointments. But he wasn't *really* prospecting because he didn't like it.

Can you identify with that situation? You may be uncomfortable with a sales activity so you don't engage in the activity. Because you don't like it, you aren't doing it. But you may be good at it! This young man, Troy, was good at prospecting. He provided the evidence that proved he was good at it. However, he was holding himself back because he didn't like it! As my daughter says, "Cry me a river. Build a bridge. Get over it!" You may have to get over some of the things that stand in the way of your sales success.

You don't have to like everything about prospecting (or selling) to be outrageously successful. You don't have to like it, but you do have to do it!

I suggest you choose six or seven selling skills and rate your proficiency for each on a separate Growth Chart. For those skills rated Consciously Incompetent, you have identified training areas on which you should focus. Remember to seek training from someone who can instruct from the Consciously Competent stage.

Selling Value Exercise

Below there are two boxes. Think of all the products or services you sell and then list three (3) things you offer in the first box. Go ahead and do so at this time. I will slow down and let you write those three things. Go on...once you have completed "what you sell," list three things your prospects want in the second box.

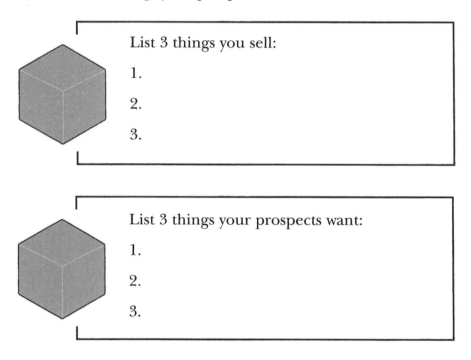

List 3 things you sell:

1.

2.

3.

List 3 things your prospects want:

1.

2.

3.

In my sales seminars, I usually walk around the room and observe the answers. This is what I often view:

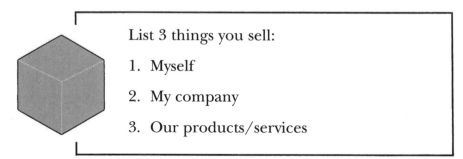

List 3 things you sell:

1. Myself

2. My company

3. Our products/services

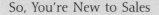

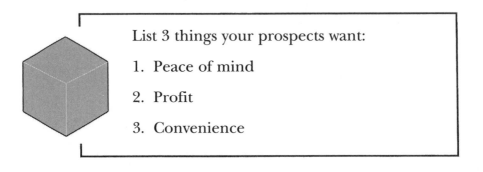

List 3 things your prospects want:

1. Peace of mind

2. Profit

3. Convenience

I am not sure what you wrote in the two boxes. However, here's the question: Do your lists match? I bet they don't! The key to successful selling is that your lists must match!!! Oftentimes, the lists don't match.

In the sales seminars, I sometimes receive a list that looks like this:

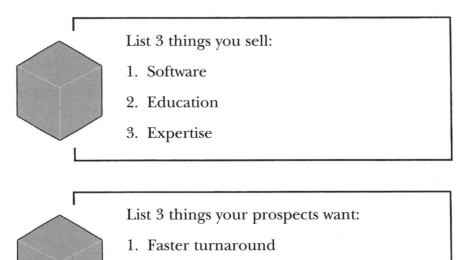

List 3 things you sell:

1. Software

2. Education

3. Expertise

List 3 things your prospects want:

1. Faster turnaround

2. Ease of installation

3. Quality service

As you can see, these two lists don't match either. If that is the case, the salesperson is going to face a challenge that is not easily overcome.

The left box – "what you sell" – is the salesperson's comfort zone. The right box is the prospect's buying zone. To be successful you must be in the same box as the prospect.

Most salespeople have a great deal of confidence in the left side. Those items listed are what most training programs drill into the salesperson. The left side is the known. That is, you know and understand what you sell and the features of what you sell. The right side is the unknown. That is, this is the side that contains the prospect's issues and concerns. In other words, you can learn about your company and its products from your new-employee orientation. You know those things. However, to understand the prospect's side you must communicate with him or her. You must use your questioning skills to uncover what the prospect wants. If your list of what you sell doesn't match the list of what the prospect wants you will not be able to provide what she needs. No sale will take place.

If you are selling insurance and the prospect wants peace of mind, you will miss the sale. The list of what you sell and the list of what the prospect wants must match! In this case, you must interpret how your prospect receives peace of mind by purchasing your insurance.

It's an easy mistake to make. In fact, I made that same mistake. When I began working for Zig Ziglar, I was living my dream. I read Zig's best-selling book *See You at the Top* and it literally changed my life. Now I found myself working for my hero! After three months with the company, Zig called me one morning and asked if I'd like to have lunch with him. I said, "Of course."

I then called Cyndi and said, "I am going to get a promotion at lunch!"

She said, "That can't be. You've only been there three months. No one gets promoted after only 90 days. You must be mistaken."

I said, "You don't understand. Zig is taking me to lunch. He doesn't go to lunch with anyone who has only been with him for that short period of time unless he likes his work. I think I am going to get a promotion."

At lunch Zig didn't talk about my promotion. Instead he talked about my performance! He said, "Flanagan, 90 days ago we forecasted your sales as being greater than they are. In fact, your sales have been rather flat."

I thought he might fire me, so I leaned forward and said, "I love you, man."

He said, "Regardless of that, what are you selling?"

I said, "I am selling books, tapes, and seminar seats."

He said, "That's the problem. We don't sell books, tapes and seminar seats."

I asked, "What do we sell?"

He said, "We provide information contained in our books, tapes, and seminar seats. If our clients take, use, and apply the information correctly, what we sell is a method to build a better self, a better family, and a better career."

I thought back to the first book I purchased by Zig, and that is exactly what I received from studying the book. I remember that I didn't really want to read a 382-page book. What I did want was to feel better about myself and increase my confidence. That is exactly what his book provided. And once I understood that, my Ziglar career took off!

You do understand why your lists must match, don't you? You aren't selling a product or a service. *You are selling what that product or service will do for that specific prospect.* In other words, prospects purchase what your product or service will do for them. They are really buying the "product of your product." Put another way, prospects buy the **results** your product or service provides to their individual needs.

Refer to the first two boxes on page 45. Write the word "Features" on the top of the first box. We usually are well-versed on the features of our products and services. We know the specifications, we understand the terms and conditions, we can demonstrate how our product performs, and how fast these functions are performed. The caution is not to explain these until you recognize what the prospect needs. Then and only then can you determine which features to address.

On the top of the second box, write the word "Values." This list describes the value the prospect is seeking. We should focus our attention on this side of the list. All of us have a natural tendency to over-explain the "features" and under-explain the "values." To be successful, you need to focus on the "values" side.

Here are three strong selling words: *values, advantages,* and *benefits.* If you can catch yourself using one of those three words with a prospect, you will know you are in a "selling mode." If you aren't using one of those three words, you are in a "telling mode." To succeed in sales, you must be in a "selling mode."

A key selling principle is:

Features — tell

Values — sell

By communicating the value, you support why the prospect should acquire your product or service. Every prospect is tuned to the old radio station WII-FM. This stands for "What's In It For

Me?" You can answer that question by communicating the value and not the features. Don't get me wrong, at some time you will have to discuss the features. But don't lead with features. The key is to **lead with need**! Lead with the prospect's need!

Your competitors have the same items as you in the first diagram. The reason prospects buy from you is found in the second. If you focus too much time on the "features" list, you will reduce your offering to a commodity. When faced with a commodity decision, people buy on price, they buy the cheapest commodity. You want to separate yourself from the competition by selling your value, your advantages, and your benefits.

Here are examples of how to use this technique when selling to a prospect's needs:

> "Ms. Prospect, our customers find great **value** in the increased productivity this system offers. These customers save both time and effort with this particular configuration."
>
> "Mr. Samson, this feature offers you several **advantages**. The first advantage is ..."
>
> "Mr. Prospect, earlier you mentioned you value greater productivity. One of the **benefits** you receive from this system is ..."

As you can see, each of these sentences highlights a *value, advantage,* or *benefit.* I suggest you make a list of similar sentences you can use to communicate why a prospect should buy from you!

Motivational Message:
The First Step in Taking PRIDE in Your Profession

Selling is an honorable profession! Of all the "helping" professions, selling ranks with the best of them. It is a top-shelf profession.

However, sales professionals have done a poor job of selling the profession to others. There is still a "stigma" associated with selling. Sometimes we hinder ourselves by identifying with the negative elements of selling. Stop it! We shouldn't fall victim to what others think about the great profession of sales. We should take PRIDE in being sales professionals. The purpose of this message, and the following five messages, is to instill PRIDE in our profession.

Let's take a look at the components of PRIDE. Each letter stands for a very specific attribute. These messages explain each letter. The following articles will then focus on each individual letter and how you can embrace your profession by embracing those attributes.

P = Professionalism. Give yourself permission to be less than perfect. Never give yourself permission to be less than professional.

R = Reserve. Sales professionals must build a mental, physical, and spiritual "reserve." It's easy to run out of gas due to your daily selling activities. Therefore, you must have something "extra" in your tank. That is where your reserve comes in.

I = Individualism. You can be yourself and succeed in sales. You've had a lot of practice being you. Use it to your advantage.

D = Development. You never graduate from selling. Spend time and money in developing your skills, your attitude, and your sales knowledge.

E = Ego Drive and Empathy. These two traits will serve you well in the sales profession. The first is the desire to solve problems (ego drive), and the second is the willingness to understand people as people and not as units of production (empathy).

I want to challenge and encourage you to embrace the attributes of PRIDE. By taking PRIDE in what you do on a day-to-day basis, you will become the professional you were meant to be.

The Sales P.R.O.C.E.S.S. Overview

Selling is a Process, Not an Event

Earlier we discussed several selling principles. The number one principle listed is **"selling is a process, not an event."** If you embrace a prospect-centered approach to your selling activities, you will out-sell the competition. You will separate yourself from the "product-centered" vendors in your industry.

Your personality will take you only so far during a sales interaction. At some point, you will need a defined process to build rapport, discover concerns, confirm needs, present a recommendation, and reach closure. It is not that your personality is not important. It is just that the process is more important. Why? Let me offer an analogy.

This is another baseball example. Here is the situation: you are facing the best pitcher in the major leagues. He has speed and control. The night you are facing him, he has his A-game; he's at his best. Are you going to step out of the batter's box and tell the pitcher a joke? No, because that will not help you at all. But that is using your personality. What you will do is this: you will adjust your skills within a hitting process so you'll have the best chance for success.

The same is true when selling to a top prospect. Are you going to "personality" your way through a sales call? Or, are you going to "process" your way through a sales call? I suggest that you use a process!

Let me answer the question you are asking at this point. You know the question you are asking, "But isn't your personality important?" The answer is yes, your personality is important. I believe the prospect buys the man or the woman before he or she buys your plan. However, your personality is not the central focus of successful selling. If it were, only a specific type of personality would achieve sales success. This is simply not the case. All types of personalities can sell. The successful ones are those who find a process that works.

Once you discover a process that works for you, selling becomes easier. That is why it is imperative to embrace a sales process.

Question: who drives the *speed* of the sales process, you or the prospect? The answer is the prospect drives the speed of the process. You must give him or her compelling reasons to either slow down the process or speed up the process. You try to control the direction of the process, but it is the prospect that drives the speed. If you have a defined sales process, it allows you to adjust to the situation more easily and more quickly.

Your frustration occurs when you expect the end of the process, while, in fact, **you** are in the middle of the process. Your mission is to join your prospect at their location and move through the process *together*.

Here is the real reason the process is so important (now pay attention, because this is almost good): Process is important because *process takes pressure off of the salesperson*! That's right. If you have a process, you lessen the pressure on yourself. You can direct the pressure off of the salesperson and onto the sales process. You can adjust your process and not change your personality.

The Importance of Process

Let's try this exercise. I must warn you, there will be some math involved in this exercise. Get ready.

Choose a number between 2 and 10.

Write the number
in the space provided: _____   (your number)

Multiply that number by 9   ___x___9___

   Total:

Add those two digits together: ____+____

Subtract 5 from this number: _____-5 =

   Total: _____

Next, equate the numeric to the alpha. In other words, assign the number to a letter in the alphabet.

Example: 1 – A

          2 – B

          3 – C

          4 – D

          5 – E

You now have a letter that corresponds to a number. Think of a country that begins with that letter. If you can spell the country's name, write it here: _____

Think of a large land animal that begins with the second letter of the country's name: _____

What color do you usually associate with that land animal?

_____

And the answer is: _____

I promise you, there are no *gray elephants in Denmark!*

What was your answer? Was it gray elephants in Denmark? Most people answer *gray elephants in Denmark.*

What is the point? The point is that I have a process. It is a process that works on any and all "prospects." It does not matter what my personality traits are. It does not matter what personality traits the prospect possesses. This will work with engineers, business owners, technicians, accountants, and lawyers (well, maybe not lawyers). The correct answer is determined by using a **process**, not a **personality**. The same is true in selling. Your sales process will carry you to greater success than just your personality.

Selling in its simplest form is a *communication process*. Yet, we tend to complicate the process. Do not make it harder than it is. Keep it simple. Baseball great Willie Mays was asked to describe the game of baseball. Willie said, "Baseball is simple. They throw it, I hit it. They hit it, I catch it." Simple. Arnold Palmer's dad taught him to play the game of golf. He said, "Son, hit the ball hard. Go find it. Hit it again!" Simple. Do not complicate selling. Selling is nothing more than asking and listening. A simple process.

The Four Sales Filters

In order for your selling efforts to be successful and for you to close each sale successfully, each process of the sale must pass through four filters. If the process breaks down at any of these four filters, a sale will not take place.

You have to sell to the right **prospect** the right **product** using the right **process** and be the right **salesperson**.

The Prospect Filter

If this person cannot make a decision, a sale will not take place. You must get to the "qualified" decision-maker. How do you determine if the prospect is qualified? Ask yourself these questions: Is this the person who can make a financial decision? Is he or she aware of the need your solution will meet? Is there a sense of urgency? The answers to these questions determine if the sale can pass through this filter.

The Product Filter

If your product or service cannot meet the needs of the prospect, a sale will not take place. Do you have the right product or service to meet the requirements of this prospect? It doesn't have to be a perfect fit, but it must meet the essential needs of the prospect.

The Process Filter

If you do not have a prospect-centered approach to selling, a sale will not take place. The process should be one that allows you to uncover existing and potential needs of the prospect. The process must involve the prospect and must engage him or her so that you generate a greater understanding of how your solutions can enhance the current situation.

The Person Filter

If you are not the right salesperson, a sale will not take place. Often, prospects buy the man or the woman before they buy the plan. Did you show up on time, prepared, poised, and focused on the prospect? Or were you running late? Did you forget the prospect's name? Did you do most of the talking? If that was the case, a sale will not take place.

The Sales P.R.O.C.E.S.S. Overview

As listed earlier, this is the Sales P.RO.C.E.S.S. Formula.

STEP	PURPOSE	HOW
Prepare, Plan, and Prospect	Get ready! Establish your call objectives	Research, observe, be open to sales opportunities, initiate contact
Relate	Build trust/rapport	Focus on the prospect
Open a Dialogue to Uncover Needs	Determine N-I-C: Needs, Issues, and Concerns	Ask appropriate questions
Confirm Needs	Gain agreement that a need(s) exists	Upset prospect's "homeostatic balance"
Explain Your Recommendation	Introduce Solution	"Let me recommend . . ."

Sell the Value	Interpret the value of your solution	Communicate from the Prospect's Point of View
Simply Ask for the Objective	Reach Closure	AAFTO: Always Ask For the Objective

Each of the seven steps in this process will be defined and demonstrated in great detail. Numerous examples will be provided so that you can modify to best fit your sales environment. Let's begin with Prepare and Plan.

Success Hint:
Selling is Asking and Listening

Selling is nothing more than *asking and listening*. You must learn to listen so the prospect will talk, then talk so the prospect will listen.

CHAPTER 3:

Prepare and Plan

The Value of Preparing and Planning

Before every NFL Super Bowl, it seems the forest animals also play a football game. It's the little animals versus the big animals. In last year's game, the big animals jumped out to a huge lead of 49-0 at halftime.

To start the second half, the big animals were to receive the ball. The mouse kicked off for the little animals. The ball sailed down to the goal line where the rhinoceros caught the ball, tucked it under his chin and took off. He had gotten only as far as the one-yard line when from out of nowhere, BOOM! The rhino was hit so hard he fumbled the ball and the ball bounced into the end zone where the rabbit recovered it for a touchdown.

The coach of the little animals was so excited that he ran onto the field and asked, "Who tackled the rhino?" The fox said, "Coach, it was the centipede!"

"The centipede? The centipede? Man, that was a great tackle!" He walked over to the centipede and said, "You are a great player! That was the hardest hit in the history of football. Where were you in the first half?"

The centipede said, "Coach, I was putting my shoes on!"

The moral of the story is: be prepared. **Preparation compensates for a lack of talent**. Preparation is a key element in successful selling. The better prepared you are, the fewer surprises you encounter during your sales day.

Here are some questions you may want to ask yourself regarding Preparing and Planning:

1. What is required of me to have a successful sales day?
2. What should be in place before I conduct my first sales activity?
3. When do I prepare for my sales day?
4. How often do I check my behavior against my goals?
5. What material/collateral/literature do I need for my sales activities today?
6. Who am I going to call on first, second, last?
7. How prepared am I to conduct an effective sales call?
8. What barriers do I have to overcome to be productive today?

The answers to these questions will determine how prepared you are for your selling day.

The Mr. Do PAT Strategy

Here is a strategy you can easily implement. It is called Mr. Do PAT. It is an acronym that stands for:

Make Ready

Do

Plan Activities for Tomorrow

Let's take these one at a time.

Mr. stands for **Make Ready**.

This simply means you must prepare for your sales day. What needs to be in place for you to have a productive day? What do you need in your car, at your desk, in your system? What should be available to you? Price sheets? Spec sheets? Online catalog? Your Customer Relationship Management software? The benefit of having things ready is that you will save valuable time and effort and energy.

Do stands for the *doing*, the actual selling activities and behaviors. These include the prospecting activities, the emails you send, the sales proposals you write, the face-to-face encounters you have, the appointments you set, etc.

PAT stands for **Plan Activities for Tomorrow**. In order to get a head start on tomorrow, you should plan those activities in advance. Prior to wrapping it up for the day, you should determine tomorrow's activities.

Key point: Preparation compensates for a lack of talent!

The 7-Step Account Planning Formula

When I was growing up, my friend Ralph had a paper route. I was too lazy to get up with him and wrap and throw the morning paper. I did, however, ask how he organized his mornings, how he determined his route. In his own humorous way, he said, "Well, I don't throw them alphabetically, I guarantee you."

That makes sense, doesn't it? Every business needs an organized system in order to achieve the best results. The same is true in selling: you must have a methodology to conduct your day-to-day activities. Successful sales professionals plan their day and work that plan. This includes strategic plans for major accounts.

The following is a 7-Step Account Strategy used in creating a plan to penetrate a major account. This strategy is powerful and thorough. By following this plan you will save time and focus your efforts on the right activities. You may have to revise or modify these steps to best fit your environment. However, this gives you a good starting point.

Account Planning Strategy

Step 1 – What are my goals for this account?

What are your goals for this account? How much business would you like to capture within this account?

The realistic potential is based upon several factors:

- Your company's history with the account
- Past purchases
- Level of customer satisfaction, etc.
- Competitive activity/installation

This information will assist you in setting goals for the account and satisfying a time frame for attainment.

Step 2 – What are the benefits of reaching this goal?

As with every other type of goal, there must be an advantage of putting forth the effort to reach it. After all, hard work must be rewarded or the goal will not receive your fullest efforts. As you work toward your goal, you will certainly encounter barriers and obstacles. By reminding yourself of the benefits in reaching your goal, you will generate excitement and motivation to overcome barriers and obstacles. List as many benefits as possible.

Step 3 – What are the major obstacles in reaching this goal?

Since you will encounter obstacles in achieving this goal, list them so you can prepare to overcome them. Being as specific as possible in listing the obstacles is not to cast a negative element on the process, but to outline the "realistic" obstacles that must be overcome. If you are going to encounter an obstacle, wouldn't you want to know about it as soon as possible? Of course you would. This is one of the benefits of listing the obstacles.

Step 4 – What skills and knowledge are required to reach this goal?

In order to reach this goal, you may have to acquire additional skills and knowledge. Create a "plan within a plan" to acquire these. Possible skill areas may include presentation skills, time management skills, proposal writing skills, etc. If time is needed to acquire these skills, accurately planning this step will assist in establishing realistic time frames. Knowledge areas may include product knowledge, competition knowledge, prospect knowledge, application knowledge, etc. List both the skills and the knowledge needed.

Step 5 – What individuals/groups/organizations can I work with in reaching this goal?

You may need to involve others in your goal. As Zig Ziglar says, "If you find a turtle on top of a fence post, you can bet he had help getting there." By identifying others with whom you will work, you can set more realistic goals and time frames for your goals. Share long-term goals with family members so they can encourage you along the way. This sharing also prepares them for the long hours and extra work necessary to achieve the goal. People within your office, such as your sales manager, may also impact or be impacted by your goals. Groups and organizations could include the marketing department, the service department, IT department, and the finance department.

Step 6 – What is your action plan for reaching this goal?

This should be the fun part of the Account Planning Strategy process! Here is where the plan takes shape in the form of "to do's" or specific tasks that are well thought out and very detailed. Invest time in this stage by setting aside a portion of your day to concentrate solely on this step of the process. To generate enthusiasm and motivation for this step, review Step #2 — "What are the benefits of reaching this goal?" Assign a deadline or time frame to each task. This will make it easier to determine the overall deadline.

Step 7 – What is your deadline for achievement?

Once you have completed the first six steps of the planning process, you will have a clear understanding of a completion date for your goal. Remember, if the date approaches for completion and you cannot complete the goal by that date, don't change your goal! Simply adjust your date.

Below are an Account Planning Strategy Form and a completed Account Strategy Planning Form. You may want to use the blank form to strategize for one of your accounts. The completed form is a guideline to assist you in that task.

Account Planning Strategy Form

Account: _____   Date: _____

Contact: _____   Contact: _____

Email: _____   Phone: _____

Email: _____   Phone: _____

Step 1: My goal for this account.

Step 2: My benefits in reaching this goal.

Step 3: Major obstacles in reaching this goal.

Step 4: Skills/knowledge required for reaching this goal.

Step 5: Individuals/groups/organizations needed to reach this goal.

Step 6: Action plan for reaching this goal.

Specific Tasks	Begin	Deadline
_____	_____	_____
_____	_____	_____
_____	_____	_____

Step 7: Deadline for achieving this goal _____

A Golf Story

Golfing great Jack Nicklaus met music great Stevie Wonder at a charity event. Stevie said, "Jack, I love golf, it's my favorite pastime!"

Jack asked, "Stevie, how can you play golf? You're blind."

Stevie said, "My caddie runs down the fairway, he yells my name and I hit the ball toward him."

Jack asked, "But, how do you putt?"

"The same way. My caddie lines me up, kneels behind the cup, he calls my name and I putt toward him."

"Wow. That's amazing, Stevie."

"Yeah, but, Jack, I only play for $5,000 a hole."

Jack Nicklaus says, "If that's the case, let's schedule a round together."

Stevie Wonder says, "Great. What **night** would you like to play?"

There are several lessons to be learned from this story.

1. Stevie Wonder had a target. He knew his target. He pursued that target. It is very difficult to hit a target you can't see. It is impossible to hit a target you don't have. Do you have a target? If not, when are you going to get one? Do you have a target for today, this week, this month? If not, it is going to be difficult for you to hit that target you don't have.

2. You may not have all the tools or all the skills necessary for success. But you can still be trained; still be encouraged to pursue your targets.

3. Attitude is important. In fact, your attitude enhances your skills. I repeat: your attitude enhances your skills. You may not be gifted with great ability, but your attitude pushes you to use what skills you do have!

Find your target. Pursue your target. Implement the Account Strategy Plan.

Sample Account Strategy Plan

Account: Texas Insurance Corporation   Date: July 9

Contact(s): Ralph Sampson   Phone: 555-469-0976

Email: rjs@tic.biz

Step 1: My goals for this account

 Upgrade our five (5) installed model 2020 with the new Abacus Series 2100

 Replace the competitive high-speed duplicators with the Abacus 9400

 Sell annual supply agreement

Step 2: My benefits in reaching these goals

 Achieve my quarterly plan

 Commission increase

 Compensate for ABC cancellation

 Qualify for quarterly bonus

 I'd be proud of my efforts

 Position us to sell company-wide

 Self-satisfaction

 Down payment on new car

 Branch office recognition

 Possible rep of the month

 Qualify for the Fall Incentive Trip

Step 3: Major obstacles in reaching these goals

 Tough competition - installed for past 10 years

 The key operators like the service technician

 Convincing my sales manager to grant volume discount pricing on supplies

 Matching the features of the high-speed duplicators

- Competition may reduce monthly usage charges once we make a formal proposal
- Budget constraints

Step 4: Skills/knowledge required for reaching these goals

- Competitive knowledge - i.e., features of their duplicators
- Analyzing past six months' invoices
- The number of long runs and amount of convenience copies per month
- Presentation skills for demonstrating our copiers
- Types of applications currently used

Step 5: Individuals/groups/organizations needed to reach these goals

- Richard - Sales Manager
- James Vale - Regional Supplies Manager
- Kathy Roberts - TI Corporation's Purchasing Agent
- Art Hanson - Field Technician Manager
- Cyndi - to understand my long hours and some Saturday morning work
- Ralph Sampson and Susan Moore (his secretary)

Step 6: Action plans for reaching these goals

Specific Tasks	Begin	Deadline
1. Contact Kathy Roberts in order to analyze six months of invoices	July 9	July 16

2. Run financial comparisons of   July 16   July 23
    current vs. proposed costs

3. Study competitive systems to better   July 9   July 20
    understand the features

4. Secure quote on annual supplies   July 10   July 16
    contract with Jim Vale

5. Schedule appointment with Ralph   July 20   July 27
    Sampson to present sales proposal

6. Practice presentation with Richard   July 19   July 20

7. Finalize presentation and proposal   July 20   July 20

Step 7: Deadline for achieving these goals

I will have the order by August 1

Motivational Message:
The Second Step in Taking PRIDE in Your Profession

The first article of this series challenged salespeople to take PRIDE in the sales profession. We assigned the following attributes to PRIDE as Professionalism, Reserve, Individualism, Development, and Ego-drive/Empathy. This message addresses Professionalism.

Professionalism

You can give yourself permission to be less than perfect, but never allow yourself to be less than professional. Nowhere is this truer than in the world of selling. Because sales pros are taught to be persuasive and convincing, we must be professional and ethical at all times. People are investing their money, their time, and their trust in you. Professionals assure others that those investments will reap a positive return.

To be a true professional, you must exhibit trustworthiness on each client interaction. One definition of trust is "meeting expectations over a period of time." A great focusing question is: how do you build trust in interactions with clients? Do you have a specific process in achieving this, or do you hope for the best? A process is better because hope is not a proper tactic. If you have trouble answering the above question, you may want to ask your mentor, or an experienced sales professional, how he or she achieves trust.

How to Demonstrate Professionalism

One effective way to demonstrate professionalism is to learn to take the attention off of you and place the attention where it belongs — on the prospect and his or her needs, issues, and concerns. Learn to ask quality questions, listen more effectively, and search for the prospect's point of view. Here's a test: After you leave a sales interview, ask yourself: do I know more about the prospect or does the prospect know more about me? You've been successful when you know more about the prospect.

Professional salespeople understand the prospect does not demand perfect; the prospect demands effective. You should concentrate on making effective sales calls, not perfect ones. The prospect does not want to see you struggle to ask the perfect question, to conduct the perfect presentation, or to use the perfect closing technique. Your prospect wants a professional who will listen to his or her needs and solve his or her problems. Perfect has nothing to do with it. Professionals concentrate on being effective!

Professionals use techniques to uncover problems in order to best serve their prospects' needs. However, sometimes techniques can be misinterpreted as manipulative. Professional salespeople understand this dilemma. They know that selling is something you do *with* the prospect not *to* the prospect. Professional salespeople understand that it is the intent behind the technique that determines professional ethics. If your intent is to serve, then you should develop effective techniques to do just that.

Your challenge is to always be professional. Never allow yourself to be less than professional.

Prospecting

Prospecting Facts

You are not always selling, but you are always prospecting.

Once again the definition of prospecting is identifying the organizations and individuals who have a potential need for your products/services/solutions.

Let's get serious about *prospecting.* Let me be candid: We make it more difficult than it is.

Here's the simplified version of prospecting:

You understand your products and services. You believe you have something to offer the prospect. You have a firm conviction your solution is better than what is being used at the present time. You believe your advantages are valuable to the prospect. You want to share these advantages with your prospect.

That's really all that prospecting is. Yet we tend to complicate it. Don't complicate it…keep it simple! It is as simple as this: you believe that you have a solution to a problem and you want to communicate that solution to a person you've never met.

Here are a few facts about prospecting:

- It's a fact that new sales professionals must build a prospect list.

- New salespeople rarely receive a listing of the best qualified prospects in the company. Therefore, you must learn to "self-generate" leads. That is, create the prospect list yourself.

- Most new salespeople don't enjoy prospecting. Oh, by the way, most veteran salespeople don't enjoy it either! You don't have to enjoy it, but you do have to do it!

- You must maintain the proper attitude to be effective when prospecting. (We will address this throughout the book.)

- Prospecting is necessary for your success. It is NOT a necessary evil, but it is a requirement for success.

- You are always prospecting. You are not always selling, but you are always prospecting. You should always be proactive in building your prospect list.

- Pressure selling is caused by a lack of prospects. The more you can add to your list of potential prospects, the less pressure you place on yourself.

- You must develop a system of identifying potential buyers.

- You must develop a process for contacting potential buyers. In fact, you may have to develop several processes for contacting your prospects.

- **Contacts lead to contracts**. Therefore, you must discipline yourself to make contacts with potential clients. You should network early, late, and consistently.

- You must have the proper attitude to be effective when prospecting. (Yes, your attitude is so important I included it twice!)

If you believe your solution will enhance the prospect's current situation, then you have every right – and responsibility — to share it with him or her.

 You will discover dozens of ways to contact your prospects. Find the ones that work for you and **implement them daily.**

Separate Rejection from Refusal

My wife, Cyndi, and I were finishing our meal at a restaurant recently when the waitress asked, "Would you like more water?" Cyndi responded, "No, thank you." The waitress smiled and went on about her business.

Let's analyze this exchange.

Was my wife saying "no" to the waitress or was she saying "no" to the waitress's offer? Cyndi was saying "no" to the offer. That is, she didn't care for any more water. The waitress did not take it personally. Part of the waitress's duties is to offer diners seated in her areas additional water, iced tea, bread, etc…When a patron says "no" (which happens a lot, I'm guessing), the waitress doesn't take it as a personal affront.

The same is true when prospecting! When contacting prospects, you should not take their response to your offer personally. Rejection is different from refusal. One is personal (rejection) and the other is professional (refusal). If you are doing your job in a professional manner and with the proper attitude, then your prospects can't put you down personally.

There are only eight people in the world that can put me down personally: my mother, my brother and sister, my wife, my two children, and my two closest friends. If you don't fall into those categories, then you can't personally reject me. Oh, you can decide not to buy my ideas…but that is professional refusal, not personal rejection. As Vice President of Sales and Training for Ziglar, Inc., I will sit at my desk and strategize on how I can get better as a sales professional. However, when I get home tonight, my wife doesn't care what you think about her husband. You see, I still have value, I still have worth.

Trust me - the sooner you learn to separate *rejection* from *refusal,* the better off you will be!

Three Elements to Effective Prospecting

There are three elements to effective *prospecting:*

1. Identifying potential prospects
2. Determining where to find prospects
3. Initiating contact with identified prospects

1. Identifying potential prospects

These are the activities used in determining on whom to call. Depending on your industry and the product or service you sell, not everyone is a potential prospect for you. Therefore, you must use some type of system to identify buyers. Here is an easy way to do so: ask yourself a series of questions that will narrow your focus. That is, ask questions so you can create a "prospect profile," i.e., the traits and characteristics of your perfect prospect.

Here are some questions that you may want to answer:

1. Who is an ideal person/organization who can benefit from my product or service?
2. What does this person look like? How old is he? Does she run her own business? Is he a homeowner? Self-employed?

3. Is this person in a position to make a decision? Can he afford my solution?

4. Does this person have a recognized, unmet need?

5. Is there a specific industry or geographical area I should target?

6. How easy will it be to schedule a meeting?

There are other questions you may want to ask. But the point is, you need to create a "profile" of your ideal prospect so that you will know what to look for in potential buyers.

2. Determining where to find prospects

Where do you find prospects? Candidly, I don't have a specific answer on this because there are so many options from which to choose.

There are various ways of finding potential buyers:

Your company database

Existing clients

Veteran salespeople in your office

Research via newspapers, local publications

Friends, families, former co-workers

Subscribe to a lead-finding service

A local networking group

Social media such as LinkedIn, Plaxo, Twitter, Facebook, etc.

There are numerous business-contact directories available for purchase. If you conduct an Internet search, you will discover there are over 771 entries of such directories; from a personalized list to customized lists to general lists. You can use various means to identify companies, industries, and people to target for your prospecting efforts.

The key is to determine a system that works for you and use it. The above-mentioned resources are tools that are available to you. You may combine several of these. It's important that you choose a resource(s) and implement it on a consistent basis.

3. Initiating contact with identified prospects

Now that you have identified the prospects, it is time to initiate contact. This can be accomplished by email, voice mail, direct mail, snail mail, etc.

However, we are going to focus on using the telephone as our instrument of choice. The following strategies describe phone prospecting. Yes, there are numerous ways to connect with a prospect. You must find one(s) that works for you. Most of us, however, must pick up the phone and make contact.

First things first: What is the purpose of the contact? You must have a clear goal in mind when preparing for the phone call.

What are you trying to accomplish? At the conclusion of the phone conversation, what information do you want to have gained? For our purposes, the objective is to schedule a face-to-face meeting.

Success Hint:
Use your Prospecting System

In his book *Why Men Hate Going to Church*, David Murrow says, "Your system is perfectly designed to give you the results you are getting." This is true of any system. It is true of your health management system, of your social system, and your family system. If the results are not acceptable, adjust your system!

The same is true of your prospecting system. If you are not generating the prospects you should be, you need to adjust your system. In other words, find a system that is effective for you and your selling environment.

Asking for Referrals

When asking for a referral, make sure you "narrow the focus" for the referring person. In other words, do not give the person the entire universe of friends and acquaintances from which to choose. Narrow the focus by asking,

> "Who do you work with that has moved into a new home in the past 12 months?"
>
> "Since you coach youth soccer, what family is new to your team? Who has moved into the neighborhood in the past year?"

By narrowing the focus, you assist the person in identifying a prospect and you increase your chances of getting a qualified prospect.

Example:

"I am trying to build my business. I am wondering if you can help me. I am hoping that you know someone who is looking for a way to increase their homeowner's protection and at the same time save money on their premiums. Who do you work with that may be in that situation?"

A Qualified Prospect

A qualified prospect is one who meets four criteria:

1. Has a recognized, unmet need

2. Has a sense of urgency to act on this unmet need

3. Has the authority to make a decision (and write a check)

4. Has the ability to pay for your product or service

Obviously, these criteria may change based on your sales cycle, your industry, your product line, etc. But these four criteria usually define a qualified prospect.

Once you've identified who to contact, the questions become, "How do I contact them? What do I say? Should I leave a voice-mail? Should I reach them via email?"

All legitimate questions. Once again, it depends on what you are selling, the type of sales cycle and sales environment, etc.

Communicating a Compelling Reason to Meet with You

One way of contacting prospects is actually lifting a telephone receiver, dialing the prospect's number, and calling him or her.

But what do you say? What words do you use? What do you say to the gatekeeper? Do you leave a message?

Before you answer those questions, you must resolve this question: What is a compelling reason for someone to meet with you? In other words, why would someone invest time with you? What is the value in taking time to talk with you on the phone and/or meet with you in person?

Once you have the answer, **you must communicate that compelling reason to your prospect.** If you articulate this reason, you will fill your calendar with appointments! No, seriously, you will. This is a very important step in building your sales success.

Remember, this prospecting call is NOT about the salesperson, it is about the prospect. Therefore, it is imperative that you focus on the prospect and not on yourself. This is easier said than done. If you follow the guidelines listed below, it becomes easier. If you work diligently at creating and revising the wording in the following formula, it does become easier.

Answer this question: What is a compelling business reason for someone to meet with you?

By meeting with me, this prospect will be able to: _____

_____

_____

Possible answers are:

- Discover solutions to costly problems
- Identify better solutions
- Make money/save money
- Save time
- Capture lost dollars
- Enhance morale
- Increase customer traffic
- Reduce expenses
- Have less stress/fewer headaches/less tension
- Provide his/her family with greater safety/security/stability

Once you determine the compelling business reason for meeting with you, you can then create sentences that convey that reason to the prospect.

Here are examples of compelling business reasons to meet with you:

1. We work with CFOs who want to capture lost dollars and reduce tax liabilities.

2. We work with agency directors to retain as many as 53% of first-year agents.

3. Our clients find value in our ability to increase their sales and build world class sales teams.

4. I work with clients who have a passion to increase their productivity while creating more family time.

The General Benefit Strategy (GBS) Formula

The General Benefit Strategy (GBS) is used to contact prospects. By preparing what to say in advance, you will gain more confidence and competence when you dial the phone. By gaining confidence, you will make more calls and you will generate more activity.

The General Benefit Strategy uses the word "general" because at this point in the sales process, you don't know the prospect well enough to state a *specific* benefit. Therefore, you need to offer a "general" benefit as a compelling reason to meet.

The more you know about your prospect, the stronger your benefit statement will be. For example, in researching your prospect, you discover he is expanding his company by opening new offices in other locations. You can use this information when creating the wording for your GBS.

The General Benefit Strategy consists of four steps:

1. Introduce yourself
2. Briefly describe the type of problem(s) you solve
3. Communicate a compelling *value-advantage-benefit*
4. State the purpose of your call

GBS Examples

"Mrs. Watts, this is Nancy with Acme Outdoor Advertising. We are a local advertising firm specializing in solving business problems caused by marketing challenges. We've assisted retail businesses such as yours in profitably promoting themselves. I would like to schedule an appointment so we could explore the benefits you can receive from our services."

Let's take a closer look:

> "Mrs. Watts, this is Nancy with Acme Outdoor Advertising." (*introduce self*)
>
> "...specializing in solving business problems caused by marketing challenges." (*problem you solve*)
>
> "We've assisted retail businesses such as yours in profitably promoting themselves." (*value – advantage – benefit*)
>
> "I'd like to schedule an appointment ..." (*purpose of the call*)

Let's take a look at another example:

> "I'm Ed Samson with Protection Services. We specialize in solving problems caused by data security issues. We've assisted insurance companies in getting confidential material off of their property and off of their minds. I'd like to meet with you and discuss the value you can receive."

Once again, this sample contained all four steps of the strategy.

"I'm Ed Samson with Protection Services." (*introduction*)

"We specialize in solving problems caused by data security issues." (*describe the problem you solve*)

"We've assisted insurance companies in getting confidential material off of their property and off of their minds." (*compelling value-advantage-benefit*)

"I'd like to meet with you and discuss the value you can receive." (*state purpose of the call*)

The GBS is flexible, meaning you can revise it to best fit your needs and your sales environment. You may find it more effective to rearrange the steps or combine steps.

"I'm Kathy Smith. I work with women in small business. They find value in our working in their business planning as well as managing their personal wealth. The purpose of my call is to schedule a time to discuss how we could work together toward achieving your financial goals. When is a convenient time to meet?"

Leaving a Voice Mail Message

You can also use the GBS when leaving a message. The object of leaving a message is to receive a returned call. By following the GBS guidelines, you increase your chances.

"I am Margaret McGowan. I represent Acme Training Company. We work with sales managers who want to increase sales results and who want to build competitive sales teams. The purpose of my call is to schedule a six minute phone call with you so we can explore the benefits your sales professionals can receive. My number is...."

Create your Own GBS

In the space provided below, create your own General Benefit Strategy:

Introduce yourself:

_____

Briefly describe the type problem(s) you solve:

_____

Communicate a compelling *value-advantage-benefit*:

_____

State the purpose of your call:

_____

The key is to create several GBS's. You may find various types of prospects within your territory. Therefore, you should have various strategies in your tool kit. Remember, this is not "first time final time." In other words, the first time you create a GBS is not the final time you create one. You must continually update and revise the GBS so that you keep it fresh and meaningful.

So let's create another one:

Introduce yourself:

_____

Briefly describe the type problem(s) you solve:

_____

Communicate a compelling *value-advantage-benefit*:

_____

State the purpose of your call:

_____

Five Creative Ways to Prospect

Selling is a contact sport. By increasing your contacts, you increase your selling opportunities. Here are five ways to contact potential buyers and build better business relationships. These may not all apply to you...but remember — this only works if you do!

1. Take a doctor jogging. One of our clients sells to hospitals, clinics, and doctors. She was having a difficult time meeting with a certain doctor. The doctor's staff told the sales rep that she (the doctor) was a jogger and that she participated in various volunteer activities within the community. The salesperson thought outside the box and entered the doctor and herself into a 5K run for "Race for the Cure." What an active way to establish a relationship!

2. Hit a bucket of golf balls. Do you play golf? (I do, but I still stand too close to the ball AFTER I hit it!) Does your prospect play golf? Instead of investing an entire four hours on the course, why don't you invite your prospect out to the driving range and hit a bucket of balls for an hour? You don't play golf? Well, try this. Pay for your prospect to receive a golf lesson by a local pro. What a swinging way to establish a relationship!

3. Celebrate obscure holidays. For instance, did you know that January is Hot Tea Month? Perhaps you know of a prospect that is a hot tea drinker. January is your month to make an impression. September is Better Breakfast Month.

Maybe you should celebrate by taking a prospect to your favorite breakfast restaurant. October is National Popcorn Popping Month. Is there an office in your territory that could use an extra large container of assorted popcorn? You'll be a big hit if you can find one. What a fun way to establish a relationship!

4. And along the same lines: Send greeting cards. Hand-written cards get opened. Hand-written messages get read. You can capitalize on obscure days because you can rest assured that you are the only salesperson celebrating these days. August 16 is National Tell a Joke Day. (Don't get me started! Did you hear about the coin collectors who got together for old dimes' sake?) September 14 is National Cream-Filled Donut Day. October 5 is National Do Something Nice Day. Buy a card. Write a message. Mail the card. Wait three days. OK, wait five days. Call the prospect and tell her you were the one who sent the card on International Tuba Day (May 7). Greeting cards can help separate you from the competition. What a creative way to establish a relationship!

5. Offer a free service. We all like free stuff. So do your prospects and their staff. Perhaps you can make a presentation in a "brown bag lunch" format. Maybe you can bring in an associate to address physical wellness, financial issues, parenting or family matters. A vice-president of a staffing agency here in Dallas conducts 30-minute sessions on what she calls "Lunch and Learn" programs. What an educational way to establish a relationship!

Prospecting should be fun and enjoyable. You have seen your fellow salespeople contact potential customers in some pretty creative ways. You can do this also. You just need to use your imagination to prospect, close sales, and help your customers. Turn on your creative machine today and have fun as you prospect!

Creative Practice

To practice your prospecting skills, try this:

Call your cell phone and leave a message. Listen to your message and ask these questions:

> Would this message motivate me to return the call?
>
> Did it sound as if it came from a professional salesperson?
>
> Was it too "mechanical"? Too "canned"?
>
> How did I feel after listening to the message?
>
> Did this person sound like a trustworthy individual?
>
> What was the compelling reason to return the call?

If you listen to your own voice, you will be able to revise your words, your voice inflection, and your sentence structure. Don't be afraid to practice. As I often say in my live seminars, "Learn in class so you are not penalized in cash!"

Motivational Message:
The Third Step in Taking PRIDE in Your Profession

This series of messages is intended to challenge salespeople to take PRIDE in the sales profession. We assigned the following attributes to PRIDE as Professionalism, Reserve, Individualism, Development, and Ego-drive/Empathy. Let's now address Reserve.

Reserve

Sales pros must build a physical, a mental, and a spiritual "reserve." It's easy to run out of gas due to your daily selling activities. Therefore, you need to have something "extra" in your tank. This is where reserve comes in.

Physical Reserve

Evidence is overwhelming that you must be in good physical condition if you are going to perform at your best in any profession, especially in selling. By being in excellent condition, you will have the energy and motivation to make that "one more call" toward the end of the day. The tired salesperson at the end of the day has a tendency to rationalize away his or her chances for being a top sales performer. Get in shape and stay in shape!

Mental Reserve

As a professional salesperson, you are going to hear the word "no" more often than other professions. You receive more feedback than other professions. Your feedback comes quick and often. Therefore, you must be "mentally tougher" than other professions. You build your mental reserve by reading good books, by listening to motivational recordings, and by attending professional training sessions. Feed your mind with the pure, the positive, and the powerful.

Spiritual Reserve

To enjoy balanced success in selling as well as in life, you need to build a spiritual reserve. Selling is a tough way to make a living! Therefore, you must have a spiritual reserve to deal with the emotional and mental demands of the sales profession. The sales profession can take a toll on your self-belief and your self-worth. Your profession can cause you to doubt yourself. Therefore, you have to be tougher than the negative situations you find yourself in at times. You need to keep the faith. Did you know that *fear* and *faith* have the same definition? That's right, they have the same definition. That definition is this: believing what you don't see is going to happen! Successful sales professionals always choose *faith!* Build your spiritual reserve by making a spiritual decision. By doing so, it will help you now and it will take the heat off of you later!

Build your **reserve** today. Remember, the most important aspect of the sales profession is you, the salesperson. Therefore, you must strive to be balanced in all three areas. The most effective salesperson is the one who is balanced physically, mentally, and spiritually.

C H A P T E R   5 :

RELATE

Separate Professional Selling from Professional Visiting

A primary skill for sales success is to establish business relationships with prospects. A key selling principle is **the prospect buys you before he or she buys your plan.** Therefore, you must become skilled at building trust and rapport.

The purpose of the RELATE step is to earn the trust of the prospect. By so doing, you have earned the right to ask questions, make recommendations, and offer solutions to problems. The key to achieving this is to "focus the attention off yourself and focus the attention on the prospect." Several skills are required to successfully complete this objective. Those skills will be addressed in this chapter.

It is important to remember the RELATE step never ends. You never complete this stage of the selling process. You are continually establishing trust with the individuals within your accounts. This is the common thread throughout the entire relationship with the organization.

It is important to build a "business relationship" and not a "friendship" with the prospect. Don't get me wrong. Friendships are important. We all need friends. However, your objectives are to uncover problems, solve those problems with your products or services, and ask the prospect to buy your solutions. I have known salespeople who establish great rapport with a prospect only to have the prospect look to the salesperson as a buddy and not as a business problem solver.

Your goal is to establish **business relationships** in order to serve your prospects. Being personable is good...as long as it leads to a positive business decision. Don't get caught in the trap of sacrificing professional relationships for personal relationships. You have to separate professional selling from professional visiting.

Three Ground Rules

There are three "ground rules" you should follow on your initial face-to-face sales call. By embracing these ground rules you can better handle the emotional demands of the sales call.

1. My prospect is more forgiving than I am. That's right. Your prospect is not as critical of you as you are! You put a lot of pressure on yourself on an initial sales call. Don't! Lighten up a bit and take the prospect and his problems seriously, but don't take yourself as seriously. You have to stop being a self-critic when you stop being fair to yourself. Give yourself permission to be successful on the sales call.

2. My prospect doesn't demand perfection, my prospect demands effective. Think about it. This prospect is giving you 15 minutes of her time. She doesn't expect you to be perfect. She wants you to be effective! If you are struggling to make the perfect sales call, it WILL NOT HAPPEN. She

knows that. She wants you to be an effective listener, and questioner, and problem solver. Notice she doesn't expect you to be perfect.

3. Give yourself permission to be less than perfect. Never give yourself permission to be less than professional.

Small Talk

There is nothing wrong with making "small talk" with your prospect. However, some prospects don't enjoy this exchange. You may be the type salesperson who is an extrovert with high energy and you enjoy exchanging social pleasantries. Your prospect, however, may be a low verbal, introverted type of person; one who is not interested in talking about the local sports team or today's weather. Therefore, you must determine how receptive the prospect is to small talk.

Making a Positive First Impression

How do you make a favorable impression when meeting someone? There are several factors.

It really begins with the reputation of your company. What has your company done in the past to build a positive impression in your community? Possible answers are:

By being a good corporate citizen

Sponsoring local events

Contributing to local charities

Funding youth sports

Hiring good people

Delivering on promises

Maintaining a high level of customer satisfaction

The question then becomes, "How do you as an individual build a positive impression with the prospect?" What we are really addressing here is your **interpersonal skills**.

What do you do to create a favorable connection when you meet someone? Here are some possible answers:

Ensure your appropriate appearance

Offer a firm handshake

Employ good posture, direct eye contact, and supportive facial expressions

Use the person's name

Respect the prospect's time (show up on time and ready for the meeting)

In his book *Silent Messages,* Dr. Albert Mehrabian claims that when speaking in a face-to-face situation and when conveying feelings and attitudes, a person communicates in this manner:

7% through words

38% through tone of voice

55% through non-verbal signals

Understand what these statistics are saying to you. When you are trying to relate to a prospect, you are really appealing to his or her feelings and attitudes. These statistics don't follow you through the entire sales interview because the entire interview is not necessarily addressing feelings and attitudes. You may be addressing logic and systems during your time with the prospect.

However, when you are trying to "connect" on an emotional level with the prospect, you should pay close attention to the non-verbal signals you are conveying.

Communication Skills

There are five non-verbal skills necessary to create a favorable impression. These are: appearance, posture, gestures, eye contact, and facial expressions.

For our purposes, the definition of appearance is "clothes **plus** your accessories that make a statement about you." It is not just your clothes, but it is also the length and neatness of your hair, the shine on your shoes, your jewelry, and how you wear your clothes. The prospect should not see you adjust your clothing during your sales interview. When standing, men have a tendency to tug at their belts or twirl their rings. Ladies have a tendency to pull up their blouse sleeves or use a hand to sweep a strand of hair behind an ear. Once you are dressed, stay dressed! Don't use distracting mannerisms that show signs of nerves or lack of confidence. You should be striving to make a statement that you are poised, confident, and in control.

There are two keys to appearance:

1. Dress **appropriately** for the person or persons you will contact. Dress appropriately for the sales situation. If the prospect's dress code is business casual, you may want to dress accordingly. However, there is some value in dressing just above the company's dress code by wearing a coat and tie. You will have to make that decision. But remember, you are trying to project an image of confidence and competency and professionalism.

2. Once you are dressed, you should stay dressed. The prospect should not witness you adjusting your tie, your belt, your shirt. Your clothes should be silent. Fight the urge to "adjust" your clothes while in the presence of the prospect.

Posture is an important non-verbal skill. If you are standing in front of the prospect and you are swaying from foot to foot, you may give the impression that you are nervous. A man can stabilize his stance by standing with feet about shoulder-width apart with his weight evenly balanced. A woman should have a narrower stance with feet stabilized. You don't want to rock back and forth or from foot to foot.

Be careful of hand movement. Your gestures should help you support the points you are making. Moving your hands just to move your hands is wasted motion. Your hands guide your prospect's eyes. Therefore, if you make a point that you can consolidate costs, you may want to use your gestures to illustrate this benefit. If you want the prospect to look at your eyes and your facial expressions, then you should leave your hands in a neutral position.

Eye contact is essential when interacting with someone. By maintaining eye contact, you are communicating that you are confident in yourself, you believe in your recommendation, and you are focusing on the other person. How long should you maintain eye contact? The rule of thumb is to maintain eye contact to the other person's comfort level. Should you interact with a confident person, he or she may extend eye contact for several seconds. He or she is telling you that long interval eye contact is comfortable. However, you may interview someone who has short interval eye contact. You don't want to appear to stare at them too long because it may be uncomfortable for the prospect. Therefore, you should use short interval eye contact with this person.

Facial expressions allow you to set the tone and mood of the sales call. By smiling, you show your comfort and your emotions. By showing a serious expression, you can communicate your intention to help solve business problems. One suggestion is to smile when you are explaining your benefits to the prospect. You can use the smile to emotionally reinforce logical benefits.

The verbal skills are also important. You can vary your pace and your volume to add impact to your sales presentation. There is a caution: be careful with vocal interference. Be careful with using distracting words and sounds. These are called "padding" sounds. Padding is the sound of the "verbal pause." They are sounds that detract from your communication. Examples are "uh, um, er, ahem, you know, I mean." These are represented by any sound, phrase, or word that when used excessively distracts and detracts from your message.

The cure to padding is silence. Don't remove an "uh" and replace it with "um." You should pause rather than use distracting sounds. A good way to break the habit is to speak in complete sentences. It is a challenge to do so, but once you do you will find your voice patterns to be more effective.

One way to cure this is to listen to your phone messages. You should do this and then determine if you would want your prospect hearing what you just said. If you are serious about elim-inating the padding, you can listen to your recorded message on the speaker device and actually keyboard what you said verbatim. Then print this typed voice message and you can see how you sound. That will get your attention! But, it will also indicate what words or sounds you use that may distract the prospect.

All the above-mentioned skills are necessary to make a positive impression. I also encourage you to visit a local Toastmasters International Club in order to increase your communication effectiveness. You can visit the website www.toastmasters.org. The site will direct you to a local club. You'll be glad you did!

Listen Up! I Said, Listen Up!

My wife says I'm not a good communicator because I don't listen — at least, that is what I think she said.

For most salespeople, listening is the time spent waiting before they get to talk again. If you want to get into trouble during a sales call, then you should spend more time talking than you do listening. If you want to be effective during a sales call, then you should listen!

Here are six methods to improve your listening abilities.

1. Resist the temptation of talking too much.

   Let's start with the most difficult one. I'm not the only sales-person who has sold the prospect and then continued to talk and actually bought the product back! You've probably talked yourself out of a sale also. Yes, at some point in the sales process you must talk more than the customer. This usually occurs in the "Sell the Value" step. However, most of the time, you should do less talking and more listening.

2. Move into the customer's comfort zone.

   The reason you talk so much is simple: by talking, you stay in your own comfort zone where you feel safe. You know more about your products or services than you do about your prospect or his or her needs. Therefore, you stay in your comfort zones longer. In order to move into the prospect's comfort zone, ask questions the prospect is interested in discussing with you.

3. Don't play "one-upmanship" with the prospect.

   This is also called "I can top that one." When you hear a prospect discuss an event, story, or experience, the tendency is to try to match his or her story with one of your own. It's alright to relate to the prospect via shared experiences if the purpose is to establish a relationship. However, make sure this tactic assists you in building the relationship, not hindering it.

4. Don't talk while I'm interrupting!

   Oh, this is a tough one. Fight the urge to finish the prospect's thoughts or sentences. Don't you find it distracting when it happens to you? So do your prospects. Oftentimes, salespeople interrupt so they won't lose their train of thought. If that's the case, design a technique to remind yourself so that you won't forget that important point. It may be a mental or written note. It may be crossing your fingers. It's okay for the prospect to interrupt you; it's not okay for you to interrupt the prospect.

5. Slow down to go fast.

   Slow down your listening. How do you do this? One way is to completely hear what the prospect is really saying. Be careful not to pre-judge. Slow down and take in all that is being said ... and what is not being said. You must know the complete problem in order to recommend the complete solution.

6. Don't be a gunfighter.

   Remember the gun fights in the old TV westerns? The gunfighter would draw his gun and fire six shots. Then, as the other guy fired his six shots, the first gunfighter would re-load. We do the same thing on sales calls. We fire all our bullets at our prospect. While he is responding to us, what are we doing? That's right ... we are re-loading. We are getting ready for our next shots ... but you are not paying attention to what the prospect is saying because you are distracted as you load your gun! This may take the form of designing your next question or mentally assessing how well the sales call is progressing. Either way, you aren't listening to the prospect. So, you should still fire your shots. Just remember to listen before you re-load. That way, you'll know what bullets to fire and you'll locate the target more accurately.

Will these six ways to become a more effective listener on a sales call work? Only if you do!

Frame the Sales Call

You have contacted the prospect, you have communicated a compelling business reason to meet with you, and you are now in front of the prospect. How do you begin the sales interview? What do you say?

You should thank the prospect for the meeting and you should "frame the sales call." That is, you should establish the direction the call should take. You should agree to the time requirement. The prospect may need to be reminded of the amount of time you requested. You can ask the prospect what direction he or she wants the call to take. By agreeing to the "frame" around the sales call, it makes for an easier transition from "small talk" to the actual sales call itself.

Here are two examples:

> "Ms. Prospect, thanks for meeting with me this afternoon. As I said over the phone, what I'd like to do is ask a few questions about you, about your firm, some of the goals you've established in the area of increasing productivity, and touch on some barriers that may be standing in the way. That will take about 15 minutes. Is that still a good time frame for us?"

> "Mr. Prospect, I really appreciate your meeting with me this afternoon. My objectives for our meeting are to get to know you, a little about your organization, and some of the challenges you are facing. Maybe tell you a bit about our firm and how we can offer solutions to those challenges. That'll take about 20 minutes. Is that a good starting point for us?"

In the space below, frame the call in your own words. What would you say if you were standing in front of a prospect who has agreed to meet with you in his or her office?

_____

_____

_____

_____

_____

_____

_____

The P.O.G.O. Profile

You have arrived on time for your appointment. The prospect greets you in the lobby, makes a few small-talk comments, and leads you to the conference room. You are seated across from him. You "frame the call" by asking for the agreed upon 20 minutes.

Now what do you do?

You should begin to ask questions so you continue to build rapport and begin to formulate a "profile" of the prospect. You conduct the interview in a conversational manner. This is accomplished by using the P.O.G.O. Profile.

The P.O.G.O. Profile is a questioning strategy that requires you to ask questions about the Person, the Organization, the Goals, and the Obstacles to achieving those goals. By understanding these four areas, you will develop a solid "profile" of the prospect and his current needs, issues, and concerns.

There are several benefits to using the P.O.G.O. Profile:

- You focus on the prospect and not on yourself
- The prospect does most of the talking
- You gain valuable information
- It gives structure to the sales call for you and the prospect
- You use your time wisely
- You establish rapport more quickly
- You gauge how receptive the prospect is
- You more easily connect with the prospect
- You establish yourself as a professional

The key to using the P.O.G.O. Profile is to become a skilled questioner. We'll address the types of questions in the chapter entitled "Open a Dialogue to Uncover Needs." The better your questions, the better the quality of the information you receive. A key selling principle is whoever has the most information has the most influence. Therefore, your questioning skills are essential.

One of the great benefits of the P.O.G.O. Profile is that it is flexible. That is, it is a fluid process. You do not have to begin with the Person questions. You can begin with any letter. For example, if you know the prospect is an analytical person who may be uncomfortable talking about herself, you may want to begin the questioning with the Organization instead of with the Person.

Let's explore P.O.G.O. Profile in more detail.

The Person of the P.O.G.O. Profile

The P in the P.O.G.O. Profile stands for PERSON. The objective is to develop a profile of the person you are interviewing. You want to ask the Person: how long has he been in this current position, how long has he been with the company, what type career he had before this company, how long has he been in the industry?

Depending on how receptive and open the prospect appears to be, you may also want to ask about the person's family, the people in the framed photos on the wall or credenza. Obviously, this is a sensitive area. Be careful how far you venture into the "personal" areas of inquiry.

Here are some examples of acceptable questions to ask:

"Mr. Prospect, how long have you been in your position?"

"What were you doing prior to this position?"

"How long have you been in the industry?"

"Where is home originally?"

"Where did you go to college?"

Depending on your industry and selling environment, you should develop Person questions that best fit your situation.

The Organization of the P.O.G.O. Profile

The first O in the P.O.G.O. Profile stands for ORGANIZA-TION. As the conversation about the person concludes, you can begin to inquire about the organization. As you discover information about her company, you can interweave elements about your own organization where you both have common ground.

You should ask open-ended questions about the organization; how it is structured, how they make decisions, etc. Your situation may dictate you ask questions about specific departments within the organization. Your situation may dictate you ask questions about the requirements of specific products or services.

Sample Organization questions are:

> "With regard to your region, how are you organized?"
>
> "What does your company require from your vendors?
>
> "How does this system fit into your overall goals?"
>
> "When do you normally shop for office space?"
>
> "How important is consistent performance to you?"
>
> "Where are you expanding to next?"
>
> "Why do you do it that way?"
>
> "How do you currently handle your advertising?"
>
> "How much territory do you cover from this office?"
>
> "Where are purchasing decisions made?"
>
> "How do you market your products?"
>
> "What is the total number of employees at this location?"

"What type of staff development are you currently conducting?"

The Goals of the P.O.G.O. Profile

The G in the P.O.G.O. Profile stands for GOALS. These questions should focus on what the prospect is trying to accomplish. Obviously, you want to ask questions about the goals you can help achieve. However, don't overlook the larger picture from the prospect's point of view. Perhaps you uncover areas that aren't in your area of expertise, but you can save money in your area that allows the prospect to fund those areas. In other words, be open to asking questions about general areas and then narrow the focus to your area of expertise.

Sample Goals questions are:

"What are your goals for the upcoming quarter?"

"What steps are in place for achieving them?"

"What are you trying to achieve with this system?"

"What role does your department play in contributing to those goals?"

"What are your benefits in achieving your goals?"

If you can assist your prospect in achieving goals, you become a hero to him or her. If you can place a prospect in a position to reach goals, you will become very valuable to your accounts. You will separate yourself from the competition.

The Obstacles in the P.O.G.O. Profile

The second O in the P.O.G.O. Profile stands for OBSTACLES. Once you determine the goals of the prospect, you need to identify what hurdles stand in the way of the prospect reaching their goals and objectives. Once again, if you assist in overcoming those obstacles, you will be a hero to the prospect.

You have to be sensitive in this area. If you don't feel you have earned the right to ask the "obstacle" type questions, you may want to wait until a later meeting to enter this area of P.O.G.O.

Sample Obstacle questions include:

"What barriers have to be overcome to reach these goals?"

"What obstacles are most crucial to overcome?"

"What steps are in place to get around that obstacle?"

"What steps have you taken in the past to overcome that issue?"

"What problem has that created for your department?"

What to Do After P.O.G.O.?

Once you have completed the P.O.G.O. questions, you can then revisit a subject that you uncovered during the questioning. You may want to use Reflective Questions to achieve this.

For example: "Mr. Watts, let's go back and discuss the consistency issue that you brought up earlier. Why is that a concern at this time?"

You will discover that the Relate step and the Open a Dialogue to Uncover Needs step overlap, they run together. As you are building rapport you will also begin to uncover the prospect's needs.

A Sales Call Using the P.O.G.O. Profile

Here is an exchange between the prospect and the salesperson. Notice how this conversation does not follow the P.O.G.O. Profile perfectly. However, the objectives of the sales call are achieved.

Sales: Mr. Watts, how is your Wednesday going?

Watts: My day is going well. And yours?

Sales: All is good. Thank you for meeting with me today. As I said, I am the Account Executive for the Western Region for Acme Outdoor Advertising. We offer a full line of services for restaurant owners such as you. However, for me to better serve you now and in the future, I would like to ask a few questions about you, your restaurant chain, some of the goals you've established to increase your business, and maybe some of the obstacles you may face. That will take about 20 minutes. Is that agenda agreeable with you?

Watts: Sure.

Sales: Mr. Watts, how long have **you** been in the restaurant business? *(Person)*

Watts: Well, like most college students, I waited tables to pay for school.

Sales: What was your major?

Watts: I actually majored in entrepreneurship. I am one of the few actually working in his field of study.

Sales: How long have you owned the Family Cooking Cafes?

Watts: We've had these for the past seven years.

Sales: Who is the "we" in your business?

Watts: My wife and mother-in-law are my partners.

Sales: What were you doing prior to operating your own stores?

Watts: I worked for a large chain. I moved around a lot, opening up various themes in different states.

Sales: How did you get back here?

Watts: I thought I had learned all I could learn. I wanted the challenge of being my own boss and seeing if I could make it on my own. I was ready to settle down back home.

Sales: So, you were raised here.

Watts: Yeah. I'm a local returning home.

Sales: Well, it seems to have worked.

Watts: Yeah, it really has. My wife and I enjoy it here. The kids seem to like it here.

Sales: According to my count you have seven stores in the area. How many people do you employ within your **organization**? *(Organization)*

Watts: Well, we actually have eight stores. We opened up the new one over on the east side last month. We average about 16 people in each store. That is both full-time and part-time staff.

Sales: And what are your *plans* to grow past eight stores? *(Goals)*

Watts: We want to expand. We have considered the franchise option. But that will take a lot of cash. So, franchising is a few years and a few dollars away.

Sales: How do you currently handle your advertising and promotions?

Watts: My wife generally handles that side of the business. We use local neighborhood mailers. She's investing in some type of viral marketing over the Internet. We haven't done a lot of radio. We can't find a station that has a focus on our demographics.

Sales: What are you trying to achieve with the mailers?

Watts: The same thing most retailers shoot for: Exposure, driving traffic to the stores, and branding ourselves. The regular things.

Sales: What **obstacles** are you facing with this advertising strategy? *(Obstacles)*

Watts: Again, it's like everyone else. We spend a lot of money on advertising and only half of it works. The problem is we don't know which half! So, we keep plugging away. But the obstacle is finding the strategy that produces the best results.

Sales: Mr. Watts, this information really helps me better understand your current situation. If your wishes could come true, what would you like to have your advertising and promotions dollars do better?

Watts: As I said, it would be nice to determine which ones are working and which ones aren't.

Sales: Why is that important?

Watts: Well, if we are going to expand or even entertain franchising, we need strong cash flow. We need more families eating in our stores.

Sales: I see. This helps me to get a better picture of Family Cooking Cafes. I would like to go back and revisit one of the statements you made earlier. You said that you were using some radio and some Internet marketing. And a lot of coupon mailers. Is that correct?

Watts: Yeah. We probably invest more in the neighborhood mailings than anything else.

Sales: How beneficial would it be if you could get greater exposure to your target families?

Watts: Of course, we'd benefit. What are you driving at?

At this point in the sales interview, you have grabbed Mr. Watts' attention and you have captured his interest. By using your P.O.G.O. Profile questions, you have actually covered the Relate step and you have entered into the next step which is Open a Dialogue to Uncover Needs.

If you review the type of questions illustrated in the P.O.G.O. Profile example, you will find they were open-ended questions. That is, the questions were worded so that the prospect would answer in an open fashion. The next chapter addresses the skill of asking questions.

Motivational Message:
The Fourth Step in Taking PRIDE in Your Profession

The first article in this series challenged salespeople to take PRIDE in the sales profession. We assigned the following attributes to PRIDE: Professionalism, Reserve, Individualism, Development, and Ego-drive/Empathy. In this message, Individualism is addressed.

Someone once said, "To be successful in sales you need to be as bold as Donald Trump, as driven to succeed as Hillary Clinton, as glib as Bill Cosby, as analytical as Bill Gates with a smile that rivals Meg Ryan's." All false! You just have to be YOU!

Individualism

That's right, just be You.

You don't have to have the same selling style, personality, or behavioral traits as Zig Ziglar, as your sales manager, or as the top performing salesperson in your office. You just have to be YOU.

You were hired because of your values, beliefs, and convictions. You weren't hired to be someone else. The only element you offer your clients that is totally *exclusive* is YOU.

You should use this to your advantage. YOU are the only unique sales advantage that you have each and every time you face a competitor. You should communicate that unique advantage each time you interact with your prospects.

There are five reasons people don't buy from you. The first four are easy to deal with. These first four are no want, no need, no money, and no hurry. As a professional salesperson, you deal with those four each and every day of your sales career. The fifth reason is the most difficult to contend with. That fifth reason is *no trust*. You can only build trust by being yourself. You earn a person's confidence by being consistent over a period of time. You win people over by sharing and exhibiting your values, your beliefs, and your convictions with them.

You have had years, maybe decades, of practicing being YOU. Use that to your advantage.

CHAPTER 6:

Open a Dialogue to Uncover Needs

Questions Are the Answer – Questioning Skills

When the salesperson was asked why she always asked questions, she replied, "Why not?"

Questions are the answer to successful selling. Questions allow salespeople to gain insights into the needs, issues and concerns of the prospect. By asking questions, you will gain information. By gaining information, you will gain influence with the prospect. The answers to your questions also allow you to build your sales presentation and solve the prospect's problem.

Therefore, it is imperative that you ask high-gain and high-impact questions in order to gain enough information to clearly identify and understand those needs. The most successful sales professionals are those who "sell by design, not by chance." If you have a strategy when asking questions, you increase your success rate.

Let me remind you of three sales principles:

1. Whoever has the most information has the most influence.

2. You are only as good as your information.

3. You make more money solving problems than you do by selling products or services.

Each of these statements is fulfilled by asking questions.

What Are You Trying to Uncover?

Before you begin to create questions for your selling activities, you need to first determine what type of information you are seeking. Once you've determined the type of information you seek, you can devise questions to solicit that information from the prospect.

Answer the following questions:

1. At the conclusion of this interaction, what do I want to know?
2. What information would be valuable to me?
3. What challenges does the prospect face?
4. How does the prospect currently address those challenges?
5. What company is the prospect presently using?
6. Who is the ultimate decision-maker?
7. How does the company/person make decisions?
8. Who has influence in the decision?
9. How price-sensitive is the prospect?
10. What is the sense of urgency?
11. Based on my knowledge of the prospect, what are the possible needs, issues, and concerns?

Once you've determined what needs you are trying to identify, you must create questions to uncover those needs. Therefore, as you learn the various question techniques, remember to create questions to address the above issues.

C.O.R.D. Questions

In order to gather information, you must become a skilled questioner. Remember, you are only as good as your information. Four types of questions will be covered. These are called "C.O.R.D. Questions." This stands for Closed-Ended, Open-Ended, Reflective, and Direct Agreement Questions.

Closed-Ended Questions

Closed-ended questions solicit facts. However, that's about the only benefit in using this type question. These are usually answered with a simple "yes" or "no." Since you receive so little information by using this type question, you may not be helped much in understanding and selling to the prospect's needs. The prospect is not encouraged to share with you any more than what you asked. If you use closed-ended questions while attempting to "uncover the need" you may not uncover all of the needs, or it may take a longer period of time to determine the real needs.

Examples of Closed-Ended Questions

"Have you used a customer relationship management system in the past?"

"Do you have a financial advisor?"

"Are you using an automated system at this time?"

"Do you rent your current equipment?"

"Did you install this (equipment) in the past year?"

"Do you consider price or productivity more important?"

"If I could meet those needs, would you purchase from me?"

As you can see, each of these questions solicits a one-word answer. Each of the answers solicits facts, but you receive no additional information!

Of course, if you are interviewing a "talkative" prospect, he may open up to you by answering these closed-ended questions in an open fashion. However, you may not know if you have an extrovert or an introvert in front of you. Therefore, you should concentrate on asking open-ended questions.

When consulting with our Ziglar, Inc., clients, I often notice salespeople who use closed-ended questions in the place of open-ended questions. Doing this too often causes the salesperson to work twice as hard to get one answer. For example, a sales rep may attempt to determine the type of insurance coverage a prospect has. If the prospect is a low verbal individual and not very talkative, the following could result:

> Sales: Mr. Prospect, do you currently have coverage in this area?
>
> Prospect: Yes, I do.
>
> Sales: What type of coverage do you currently have?

In the above example, the salesperson had to ask two questions in order to obtain one answer. The salesperson could have asked one open-ended question and received the answer he/she was seeking. Even if the prospect had no coverage at all, the sales rep would have received the answer by asking an open-ended question.

> Sales: Mr. Prospect, what type of coverage do you currently have?
>
> Prospect: I am not carrying any coverage at this time.

Most closed-ended questions can be turned into open-ended questions by placing one or two words in front of the question or by rearranging the words. For instance: in the above example, the original question was, "Do you currently have coverage in this area?" By adding one word and rearranging the others you have a much better question: "What is your current coverage in this area?"

A key point is to word the questions in a way that the answer gives you the information you are seeking. If you are seeking facts or short-to-the-point answers, then closed-ended questions are best suited. If you are seeking more information than just facts, you want to use information-seeking questions. You would then use open-ended questions, which will be covered next.

Listen to yourself ask questions. Tune into your questioning skills so that you can improve upon this vital aspect of successful selling.

Open-Ended Questions

Open-ended questions are the most valuable type of question because they solicit the most information. In selling, you are only as good as your information. The better your questions, the better the information you gather. The better your information, the better your chances of understanding what is important to the prospect.

Selling is not telling! Selling is asking and listening to the answers.

When we salespeople talk too much we move into the "telling zone." When we ask and listen, we move into the "selling zone." You make more sales in the "selling zone" than in the "telling zone."

As sales professionals, we know we should ask questions. It is logical. However, we don't always follow this logic. Here is an idea that may assist you in your selling activities today.

The focus of the question should be on the prospect, not on the salesperson, the product, or the service. Here is an example of the focus of attention being on the salesperson: "Mr. Prospect, if my system can save you money, will you buy from me?" What is the last word in the question? The word "me" — meaning the salesperson. You should focus on the prospect, not on yourself. Your questions should focus on the prospect by asking questions about him.

We can focus the attention on the prospect as well as receive valuable information by wording the question differently.

Let's try this: "Mr. Prospect, if this system can save you money, what's the benefit to you?" Now, what is the last word of the question? That's right, the last word is "you" — meaning the prospect. Now the attention is squarely on the prospect and his benefits. The answer reveals the value and the advantage to him in acquiring a new system.

Examples of Open-Ended Questions

You should create a series of questions that best suit your selling situations and challenges. However, questioning skills don't work unless you do. Here are some examples – notice the use of question words: what, how, where, when and who:

> "If you had these security features in your home alarm system, what's the benefit to your family?"
>
> "By controlling the maintenance costs, what's the benefit to your department?"
>
> "Mr. Prospect, what criteria did you use in selecting your current coverage?"
>
> "Where are you currently going for maintenance?"

"Who other than yourself is involved in the evaluation process?"

"How does your system operate?"

"What steps are in place to achieve the goals you just outlined?"

"For what reasons did you convert to that system?"

"How often do you change vendors?"

"If you had better coverage for a lower premium, what would be the benefit to you?"

"What is the advantage to you?"

"When does your lease option expire?"

You must condition yourself to ask the right questions and then allow the prospect to answer. Here is a common mistake. We ask a good open-ended question...and then ruin it by turning it into a multiple-choice question!

Example: "Why did you convert to that system? I mean, was it because of speed, ease of operation, or cost effectiveness?" We just turned a good, solid open-ended question into a multiple choice question! The prospect could simply answer by replying, "B" — meaning "ease of operation" — your second choice. The original question, "Why did you convert to that system?" gives the prospect a wide range of answers from which to choose. By asking, "Was it speed, ease, or cost effectiveness," you have narrowed the range of answers to only those three choices! Don't do that! Ask the question and let the prospect answer.

If the prospect hesitates in answering the question, you may need to assist him with possible answers. Here is an example: Suppose the prospect hesitates when you ask, "For what reasons did you convert to that system?" He may not know how to answer your question.

You may then want to assist in the answer with: "The reason I ask is that several of my clients have made similar decisions based on speed, ease of operation and cost effectiveness. I was wondering what criteria you used in your decision." You have given him time to think and you have provided him areas to think about.

Condition yourself to ask open-ended questions and let the prospect answer.

Remember: questions are the answer to "How do you sell effectively?"

Reflective Questions

Reflective questions are really open-ended questions that are used to "reflect" on a previous comment or answer given by the prospect. These are used in the "uncover the needs" step of the selling process as well as in overcoming objections or resistance. They are also used to encourage the prospect to expand and/or expound on a previous comment. This allows you to gather additional pertinent information.

There are several benefits to reflective questions:

- They allow the salesperson to control the direction of the sales call.
- They allow the salesperson to dig deeper by asking the prospect to expound or expand upon a previous answer.
- They establish trust between the prospect and the salesperson because the salesperson must be paying attention to the details of the conversation in order to ask a reflective question.
- They allow the salesperson to capture valuable information.

They can be used to encourage the prospect to emphasize a point previously made.

Usually, reflective questions are based on prior comments of the prospect. For example, the prospect may have said, "I'm fairly pleased with our current coverage." You may want to use a reflective question such as, "Mr. Prospect, what do you mean you are 'fairly' pleased?" The answer may give you insights into how to replace the current coverage.

Examples of Reflective Questions

"You mentioned earlier that your organization is cutting back on expansion plans. Why is that?"

"You said that your revenue growth didn't keep pace with past years. What were the contributing factors?"

"Earlier you mentioned expanding into new markets. How are you going to fund the expansion?"

By asking the prospect to comment on a previous answer, you may obtain vital information to move you closer to the sale! Reflective questions allow you to do just that.

Direct Agreement Questions

Direct agreement questions are asked to obtain agreement. These are typically "yes/no" answered questions, but asked in situations where you already know the answer to the question! The benefit is that the prospect's answers support your product, service, and/or your recommendation. You secure agreement with the prospect by using this type question. That's beneficial to you, isn't it? (The last question is an example of the direct agreement question.) You should use these when asking for commitment and for closing the sale.

Examples of Direct Agreement Questions

"Ms. Prospect, you mentioned earlier you wanted a durable and long-lasting solution. You do agree this model meets that criteria, correct?"

"Since you see the value of our solution, shouldn't we go ahead and schedule your shipment?"

"Mr. Prospect, that's a good fit, isn't it?"

"Don't you agree this meets your needs in those areas?"

"You could save time by placing the order, couldn't you?"

"So, quality is more important than price?"

"After the demonstration, you agreed our system meets your needs. Is that correct?"

"Mr. Jones, you are ready to schedule installation, aren't you?"

You will have to formulate these questions to best fit your selling situation and selling challenges. It is suggested that you even write a list of questions so that you can be more comfortable and effective when asking them. If you could be more effective in your questioning skills, that would be valuable to you, wouldn't it? (Again, another example of a direct agreement question!)

Replacement Selling Questions

As a new salesperson, you may receive a territory or a customer base that contains the installation of competitive products or services. If that is the case, you will need skills in the area of "replacement selling." You are either growing your existing accounts or you are replacing an incumbent competitor. This section addresses how to replace the incumbent.

In those situations where a competitive product is installed, the prospect is probably pleased with the performance and/or service she is receiving. Your challenge is to persuade her to give you the opportunity to demonstrate the superiority of your product or service.

This is accomplished by asking a series of questions. However, these questions must be structured so that you can have a fighting chance. In the past, a sales rep would only ask a few questions, determine that the prospect was content, and promptly end the sales call. Let's use a series of questions that encourage the prospect to become open to your recommendation.

The following illustration is one strategy of "**replacement selling**."

Mr. Watts, I understand you are currently using Brand CBA. What do you like about the service you're receiving? "*I like everything.*"

Well, what do you dislike about it? "*Nothing.*"

If you could wave your magic wand and change one or two things, what would they be? "*Well, like I said, I really like it all. Nothing to change.*"

(If the prospect says he's happy, what do you do? Do you end the call and go to the next one? Or, do you stay and fight one more round by asking...)

Mr. Watts, how long have you used Brand CBA? "*About 18 months.*"

And what were you using prior to that? "*It was Brand B.*"

When you made the switch 18 months ago, what criteria did you use in making the decision? "*The three most important areas for us are service, cost effectiveness and ease of use for our technicians."*

How have those criteria changed over the past 18 months? *"They haven't."*

So those criteria haven't changed. These are still important to you. How beneficial would it be for you and your department to receive service that will meet that criteria, maybe even surpass it? *"Well, we are always looking for ways to improve."*

Mr. Watts, I'm confident we can exceed your criteria.

The purpose of this questioning strategy is to create enough interest so that the prospect will at least be receptive to hearing your recommendation. That's the purpose of "fighting one more round" by using replacement questions.

The key is identifying the prospect's criteria. By doing so, you can leverage your strengths by comparing the present situation to your superior benefits.

Practice Specific Questions

You now need to formulate specific questions to ask. Here's the situation: you have an appointment with a prospect you have not yet met. He's agreed to a 15-minute meeting with you. Your assignment is to list questions you may ask when meeting with him.

Examples:

What challenges are you currently facing?

What product do you currently use in this area?

What expectations do you have of vendors?

How familiar are you with our company?

What criteria do you use in making decisions in selecting a system?

Who/what is involved in your decision-making process?

List your questions below:

_____

_____

_____

_____

_____

_____

CHAPTER 7 :

Confirm Needs

Where Is Your Focus?

In my youth, I dated a young lady who made me feel as if she were the <u>only girl</u> in the world. On May 7, 1966, I had a date with Cyndi Kadi. She made me feel as if I were the <u>only boy</u> in the world. Cyndi and I have been married 40 years.

Where do you focus your attention? Do you focus on yourself or on the prospect? I suggest you focus on the prospect! I am glad Cyndi did.

This step of the Sales P.R.O.C.E.S.S. requires both you and the prospect recognize and confirm that a need exists. Your goal is to have the prospect confirm verbally that he is aware of a better way to do things. This will lead to your being able to recommend a solution.

There are seven elements in achieving this. You must understand:

1. The difference between ache and pain
2. The term "homeostatic balance"
3. The light bulb analogy
4. How you, the salesperson, recognize the prospect's need
5. How to assist the prospect in becoming aware of his/her need

6. The questions to ask to create awareness

7. How to gain confirmation from the prospect that a need exists

Ache Versus Pain

How much money do you make on the sales you *almost* close? I mean when you get really close? When the prospect is about to sign the agreement, or is about to say "yes" but suddenly changes her mind. How much money do you make when the sale is that close?

That's right...you make the same amount of money as I do on the sales I almost close — zero, nada, zip!

So, do you ever wonder why you don't win more of the "close ones"? The answer may be the difference between "ache" and "pain."

Most prospects don't take action until they are in enough "pain" to change their current situation. In other words, the prospects' proverbial light bulbs are not fully illuminated. They may have some discomfort; they may have some pain. But they are not hurting enough to discontinue using the incumbent competitor and switch to your company. Perhaps this story will illustrate the point.

Two West Texas ranchers were talking one afternoon. The visiting rancher noticed his friend's dog lying on the porch. The dog was moaning. He asked, "Why is your dog moaning?" The answer, "Well, he's lying on a nail. But he's not in enough pain to move!"

Until your prospect is in "enough pain to move" (to take action), the prospect will not change and will not agree to buy your product or service. Your challenge, as a sales professional, is to uncover the prospect's pain. In order to achieve this, you must assist the prospect in becoming aware of the existing needs, the existing "pain." This is achieved by asking appropriate questions.

These questions are intended to move the prospect from being in an "ache position" to a "pain position." Once the prospect is in pain, your chances of winning the business are increased. Another way of explaining this is to understand the term "homeostatic balance."

Homeostatic Balance

The natural law of "homeostasis" states that an organism stays in balance until and unless acted upon by an outside force. The outside force causes the status quo to be disrupted, and the organism becomes out of balance. When out of balance, the organism realizes this and takes action on returning to balance.

The same is true for your prospects. Prospects rarely take action until and unless they are OUT OF BALANCE. Once out of balance, action will be taken to return to balance.

One of your objectives is to help your prospect realize there is a better way to satisfy her needs or solve her problems. That is, your solution will provide better advantages than her current situation.

If she is satisfied with the current situation (in other words, she is in balance), this does not mean you can't provide more satisfaction in meeting those needs. This does not mean you can't provide a solution that enhances her current situation. You have to identify her current needs and how they are being met. Once you recognize the needs and you become aware of those needs, your job is to create need awareness on the part of the prospect.

Be careful during this step of the selling process. This is often where the sale is made or lost. If you don't take your time in this step, you may frustrate the prospect and lose the sale.

Illuminating Two Light Bulbs

The purpose of the Confirm the Need step is to confirm that a need exists. Both the salesperson **and** the prospect must have an awareness of those needs. If you don't have "need awareness," you will not know what solution to recommend. If the prospect doesn't have "need awareness," he will continue to use what he has been using in the past.

This is the tricky part of the sales process. You must clearly recognize that a need exists. So must your prospect! He or she must also recognize a need exists, accept the fact a need exists, and acknowledge a need exists. You should not move to the next step of the process until and unless the prospect recognizes and agrees that a need exists. Because this is often the tricky part of the sales process, several examples and analogies will be used to cover this very important aspect of sales.

When uncovering the needs of the prospect, there are two dynamic factors occurring. These are the "awareness" factors. BOTH you and the prospect must be fully aware of the needs before you start to satisfy that need.

To assist in understanding this awareness, let's use a light bulb analogy. A light bulb must be fully illuminated in your mind as well as in the mind of the prospect to indicate a conscious "awareness" of a need.

Light Bulb 1 – Salesperson Awareness

The first light bulb represents the SALESPERSON's awareness of a need. You, the salesperson, have uncovered the real needs, issues and concerns and you are now aware of them. As you are asking questions and talking with the prospect, a light bulb goes on in your mind signifying that you understand the need. You might say to yourself, "Oh, now I understand what she is saying!" Or, "Yes, I understand what he needs." If you don't have this awareness, you won't know what to recommend. You can't move to the Sell the Value step until you have clearly determined in your mind what the prospect needs. You become aware of the prospect's needs by asking questions to gain knowledge. Knowledge is power! You need to know about your product, your industry, your competition, your pricing, as well as the prospect's buying criteria, etc.

Light Bulb 2 – Prospect Awareness

Obviously, there are two people involved in this process – you *and* the prospect. The second light bulb represents the PROSPECT's awareness of a need. Therefore, the PROSPECT must reach a point of need-awareness. The light bulb must be illuminated in his mind before he is willing to change. If not, he won't buy from you because in his mind there is no reason to do so. In order for that to take place the prospect must be upset with the current condition. Then, and only then, will the prospect take action.

If we follow the light bulb analogy, when the light bulb is fully illuminated in the mind of the prospects, their homeostatic balance is upset. The prospects will then take action to return to balance. Your objective is to help return them to balance.

How Do You Recognize the Prospect's Need?

As the prospect is answering your questions, you must tune in to their responses. By doing so, you'll be better suited to relate your solutions to his or her needs, issues, and concerns. To recognize the prospect's need, you should have knowledge in the following areas:

Product Knowledge	Competitive Knowledge
Industry Knowledge	Prospect Knowledge
Application Knowledge	Pricing Knowledge
P.O.G.O. Knowledge	Buying Criteria

By relating your knowledge to the prospect's responses you are in a better position to recognize and understand the needs from the prospect's point of view.

Answer These Questions

You may also gain an understanding of the prospect's needs by asking yourself these questions. Fill in the answers in the space provided.

1. How do I recognize a prospect's need exists?

_____

_____

_____

2. What verbal indicators should I look for?

_____

_____

_____

3. What non-verbal indicators should I be aware of?

_____

_____

_____

4. What questions should I ask to confirm the prospect acknowledges a need?

_____

_____

_____

Assisting Your Prospect in Recognizing a Need

How do you assist the prospect to become aware of the need?

Sometimes the prospect has "need awareness" before you do. His situation gets to the point that he is upset with his status quo. For example:

A person driving an eight-year-old car may discover the cost of repairs is more than the car is worth. She begins to shop around for a new automobile.

A person has not been taking care of himself physically and wants more energy and less weight. He walks into a health club to inquire about a membership.

The business owner notices a lack of productivity due to a lack of proper use of company software. He contacts a local consultant to turn things around through training courses. His action indicates he has an awareness of a need.

The above are examples of prospects becoming out of "balance" due to their situations. In these cases, the "outside force" may be outside the prospect's span of control. In the examples above, the outside forces could be the condition of an automobile, or the difficulty in fitting into a current wardrobe, or a realization of a decline in productivity. Regardless of how he got out of balance, he is taking action on the need by initiating contact with a salesperson.

Let's suppose a prospect calls you and invites you to submit a bid or proposal. In this situation, she already has need awareness. She realizes she is out of balance and is taking action to return to balance. In this case, the sales cycle is much shorter and some of the steps have already been completed.

However, if you proactively call on the prospect – if you initiate the contact – it is a good bet that the prospect doesn't realize she has a pressing need or problem. The need may exist, but it has not gotten to the point where the prospect is aware of it. The need may lie just below the surface. In this situation, the sales cycle is much longer. This also requires more involvement on your part to help her become aware of the real need and to give her a sense of urgency to take action on that need.

How do you do this? Once you've recognized the need, you ask questions. At first, you may be uncomfortable asking some of these questions. Although these questions make you uncomfortable, if they are effective, you should ask them.

You may then want to VERIFY the importance of the need by asking, "How beneficial would it be if you could correct your present situation?"

And you may want to GAIN AGREEMENT that there is interest on her part to change or take action by asking, "You are interested in improving that aspect of your business, aren't you?" Or, "You do see the value in correcting that issue, don't you?"

Questions to Create Prospect Awareness

Yes, you are going to encounter prospects that seem to be satisfied with their present situation. They are in "balance." Your objective is to determine if you have a better solution than the one they are currently using. In this situation you, the salesperson, become the "outside force." To achieve this, you must gather enough information to understand how he is currently solving his problems. Once you have awareness, you can ask open-ended questions so that he can begin to accept there may be a better way to address his situation.

The best method to create awareness on the prospect's part is to ask questions. The following are ideas on questions to ask. Some of these questions may seem a bit straightforward. But remember, by the time you get to this stage of the process, you have invested time in building the relationship, asking questions, identifying needs, and realizing that you have a solution to offer.

"Mr. Prospect, if you could improve your current situation, what would be the benefit to you?"

"Mr. Prospect, how satisfied are you with your current situation? Are you dissatisfied enough to take action today?"

"Mr. Prospect, if you could receive great protection at lower premiums, what would be the benefit to you?"

"Mr. Smith, you would agree that reducing your monthly premiums would be a good business decision, wouldn't you?"

"Mrs. Watts, you mentioned earlier that increasing the workflow productivity is a priority. How open would you be to a presentation on how to achieve this?"

"Tom, you seem to be satisfied with ACME software. What would be the benefit if you could exceed the standards you mentioned earlier?"

"How satisfied are you with ACME software? Are you dissatisfied enough to explore more efficient solutions?"

The purposes of these questions are to help the prospect realize he has a need and to help him understand there may be a better way to solve his problems. These questions are an attempt to upset the prospect's status quo (get him or her out of balance) so that you can present a better solution. These questions are also intended to have the prospect confirm he or she recognizes a need.

Confirm the Prospect Has a Recognized Need

Once you have enough information regarding the prospect's need, once you have awareness on your part, you can then confirm the prospect also has awareness of his or her need. The following question is used to confirm this awareness.

"Mr. Jones, you said earlier that your present insurance coverage is satisfactory. You also mentioned you were trying to save money in your monthly expenses. If you could combine your premiums and receive a volume discount as much as 37%, how beneficial would it be to you?"

The purpose of this question is to confirm with the prospect a better way to save money on monthly premiums. The purpose is to make the prospect aware that there is a better way to pay for insurance protection. If he answers by telling you the benefits of saving as much as 37%, he has awareness, the light bulb is on, and he is out of balance. You can then recommend a solution.

Motivational Message:
The Fifth Step in Taking PRIDE in Your Profession

The first message in this series challenges salespeople to take PRIDE in the sales profession. We assigned the following attributes to PRIDE as Professionalism, Reserve, Individualism, Development, and Ego-drive/Empathy. In this message, we'll address Development.

Development

You never graduate from selling. All professionals invest time, energy, emotion and money in developing their skills, attitudes, and knowledge about their profession.

Zig Ziglar is a great role model for us all and for a lot of reasons. One of the main reasons is that he is a constant learner. Every Monday morning, we conduct a 30-minute devotional at Ziglar headquarters. (And, if you are in the Dallas area, you are invited to attend...just show up, sit in the audience, listen to the presenter for the morning, and meet the Ziglar staff.) If Zig is in town, he attends our devotional and he always sits in the front row, stage right with a pen and pad of paper in hand. He takes notes on what the speaker has to say. Now, here's a man who has written 29 books and has touched countless lives with his philosophy. When he speaks, we should be taking notes on what he is saying. Yet, there he sits, taking notes and continuing to learn and develop. What a great role model for all sales professionals! Zig understands that you never graduate from learning. We all need to follow his example.

Develop Your Skills

Professionals invest in their selling skills and techniques. They study, read, listen, observe and ask questions about their profession. Here's a great technique I learned from one of the most professional saleswomen I've ever met. While managing a sales team at IBM, I was in charge of announcing a new product. I asked Mary to give me the top five prospects she was going to call on after we announced the product. She refused to give me her top five prospects. When I asked why, she taught me a great technique that I still use to this day. She said, "Bryan, I don't call on my top five prospects when new products are announced. I call on my *bottom five prospects!* Those prospects aren't going to buy from me anyway. By calling on these prospects first, I learn how to sell to the accounts who will buy." What a great lesson to learn!

Develop Your Attitude

I am a big baseball fan. I believe baseball teaches us great sales lessons. One of my favorite players was Ernie Banks of the Chicago Cubs. Ernie never won a world championship. In fact, at one time he held the major league record for most games played without ever playing in a World Series. Did that negatively impact his attitude? No! Ernie was known as Mr. Cub and he was also known for his positive attitude, his love of the game, and for his favorite expression: "Let's Play Two!" What a great attitude and what a great example for all of us. You may not win every sale, but you can have a winner's attitude.

Develop Your Knowledge

It is a given that you should have product knowledge. Let me suggest that you should gain enough knowledge about your products or services so that you develop a **strong passion** for what you sell. Zig says that selling is nothing more than "transference of feeling." If you can transfer how you feel about your products or services to the prospect, you will have a customer for life. How do you develop this passion? You need to see the benefits of your products or services in action. If possible, you need to actually use your products or services. This will give you a first-hand, personal feel for the advantages you offer. If that is not possible, you should visit a satisfied customer and observe how your solutions contribute to the success of your customer. Suggest that the customer write you a testimonial letter bragging on your company. That should really light your fire and spark your passion for your solutions (if it doesn't, your kindling is probably wet). Remember, you never graduate from selling. Take the time and effort to develop your skills, your attitude, and your knowledge.

CHAPTER 8:

Explain Your Recommendation

Transition

The purpose of this step is to transition to the Sell Your Value step. This step is brief and to the point. It can be completed in three sentences.

At this stage, you want to transition from asking questions to actually making the sales presentation. You should ask permission to move to the next stage by asking, "Mr. Watts, we both agree that there is a better way to address these issues. That's correct, isn't it? May I recommend we now discuss a way to solve these challenges for you?"

When you explain your recommendation, you must relate the information that you gained during the earlier stages of the sales process. Here is an example of a process entitled BIC. It goes like this:

- Based on . . .
- I'd Recommend . . .
- I'm Confident . . .

"Mr. Watts, <u>based on</u> what you've said so far and the problems you are experiencing, <u>I'd recommend</u> that you install the Model 101. <u>I'm confident</u> that it will exceed your expectations."

You should modify this strategy so that it fits your sales environment.

"Mr. Watts, we've spoken about your current challenges in the area of productivity and recapturing lost clients. Based on those challenges, I'd like to recommend a solution that will return your initial investment within three quarters. My team and I are confident you can return your investment and reach your growth projections of twenty-two percent."

Again, this step is preparing the prospect to receive your presentation.

Practice Your BIC

In the space provided below, write a BIC statement. Choose a real prospect and/or a future prospect and create your statements.

Based on _____

I'd like to recommend _____

I am confident _____

You may have to create several of these statements to fit your situations. You may discover you can modify the above method to have more impact on your prospects.

Motivational Message:
The Sixth Step in Taking PRIDE in Your Profession

The first message in this series challenged salespeople to take PRIDE in the sales profession. We assigned the following attributes to PRIDE as Professionalism, Reserve, Individualism, Development, and Ego-drive/Empathy. In this, the final article of the series, we'll address Ego-drive and Empathy.

Professional salespeople take PRIDE in themselves and their profession. Professionals are driven to succeed. They work diligently to solve problems and they are focused on results. At the same time, professional salespeople are concerned about the well-being of their prospects. These salespeople develop a deep empathy for prospects and their challenges. This leads us to the last attributes of PRIDE: Ego-drive and Empathy.

Ego–Drive

Ego-drive shouldn't be confused with conceit. This attribute is a motivation to achieve success in the sales profession. However, it is more than just a determination to win. It is also a determination to prepare, plan, and position yourself to win. Yes, this includes being competitive and driven, but not to the detriment of others. Ego-drive is bringing others with you as you succeed.

Empathy

When you tie empathy to ego-drive there is very little danger that you are going to oversell or over-promise. With empathy, the sales professional understands the client's problems and knows exactly how the prospect feels. But because you don't feel the same way, you have the perspective of backing away from the problem and offering positive solutions. Many sales professionals develop a way to move comfortably from the seller's side of the table to the buyer's side.

Psychologist H.M. Greenberg emphasizes if you are going to build a successful business career, in addition to ego-drive, you must also possess empathy for the prospect. When we separate the word *business* into its component letters, B-U-S-I-N-E-S-S, we find that the U and the I are both in the word. In fact, if U and I were not in business, it would not be *business!* If you look a bit closer, you will discover that the U comes before the I in business. On even closer observation, you'll also notice that the I is silent. In other words, it is to be seen, not heard. For you to build your professional sales career, you need both the U — the prospect — and the I — the salesperson.

Sales professionals understand this and act on being ego-driven as well as becoming empathetic toward their prospects.

Embracing the attributes of PRIDE — Professionalism, Reserve, Individualism, Development, and Ego-drive and Empathy will result in sales success!

Sell the VALUE

Computers Are a FAD!

That's right! Computers are a fad! They will disappear. They will go by the wayside. They will have the same fate as dinosaurs. They will go out of style.

However, what computers <u>do</u> for you will never go out of style.

What do computers do? Computers help you save time. They help you save money. They provide you with entertainment. They make your life easier. If another invention comes along that offers better time and money savings, you will leave your old computer behind and invest in the new technology.

You see, we don't want computers — <u>we want what computers do for us</u>! We want the "solutions" computers offer. We want the values, the benefits, and the advantages of computers.

Your prospects are the same. They want what your products and services <u>will *do* for them</u>. When solving your prospect's problems and challenges, you should concentrate on selling "solutions," not on your particular product or service.

We now address how to sell the value of your solution.

Where Are You in the P.R.O.C.E.S.S.?

Let's get caught up on where you are in the **P.R.O.C.E.S.S.**
So far:

> You planned and prepared for the call **(Plan and Prepare)**
>
> You set the appointment for a face-to-face interview **(Prospect)**
>
> You conducted the interview, related, and established rapport **(Relate)**
>
> You opened a dialogue and discovered needs, issues, and concerns **(Open a Dialogue to Uncover Needs)**
>
> You confirmed the prospect recognizes a specific concern **(Confirm the Needs)** and is off balance enough to hear your recommendation **(Explain your Recommendation)**

It is now time to conduct a sales presentation to communicate why your solution best fits those needs, issues, and concerns. This is the *Sell the Value* Step.

Remember one of the key selling principles: you make more money solving problems than you do by selling your products. This is the step in which you demonstrate how you can solve problems.

Features – Functions – Bridge – Benefits

When selling your value, you should interpret the "value" of your products or services using the Feature/Function/Bridge/Benefit formula. The presentation of the solution must be made from the prospect's point of view using these four categories.

So, how do you introduce a solution? The key is to personalize the solution for your prospect by stating the BENEFITS of your product or service.

In presenting your solutions you must ask yourself, "What's in it for this prospect?" The answer to this question is different for each prospect. In order to answer the question, you must completely understand the needs of the prospect. And you must understand this from the prospect's point of view.

Here is an example of communicating the value to a prospect.

> "Mr. Prospect, you have identified your needs to be: easy to use, fast, and able to handle a high volume of work. You have also stated that in making your decision you will consider cost effectiveness. Is that correct?
>
> "Here is how my Model 3330 best meets those needs. Our Model 3330 has a clearly-identified duplex feature button. This allows your staff to make copies on both sides of a sheet of paper. The benefit to you and your staff is the ease of using just one button for your copying application. Another benefit you will enjoy is that you will save money in paper and time by copying on both sides of the paper."

Definitions

Prospects buy what your products or services will do for them. In other words, your prospects buy the "product of your product." They buy the benefits of your solutions. Too often salespeople do not fully understand how to clearly interpret the benefits. In order to achieve this, you must be able to differentiate between *features, functions,* and *benefits.*

Let's define each of these terms and then apply these definitions to several examples.

<u>Feature:</u> A feature is a trait, a detail, or a characteristic of your product or service. A feature is a fact about your

product or service. The feature produces the benefits for the user. Only the features that produce meaningful value are useful to the prospect.

For a tangible product, a feature could be what the product is made of, how it is made, the design pattern, the color, etc. For an intangible service, a feature could be the length of the contract, the warranty, the terms and conditions, the amount of coverage, the location, the pricing structure, etc.

Function: A function is the act performed by the feature. The function is tied directly to the feature. Another way of defining the function: it is what the feature does.

Bridge Statement: The bridge statement connects, or bridges, the feature and the function to the prospect's benefit. It is a short phrase, usually less than six words, that prepares the prospect to hear the benefit.

Benefit: A benefit is the advantage in using the feature and the function. A benefit is the advantage received for using the feature versus not using that feature. Prospects want meaningful benefits which assist them in achieving an objective.

Let's dissect the example used earlier. Notice how all four components were used in communicating the benefits:

> "Mr. Prospect, you have identified your needs to be: easy to use, fast, and able to handle a high volume of work. You have also stated that in making your decision you will consider cost effectiveness. Is that correct?

> "Here is how my Model 3330 best meets those needs. Our Model 3330 has a clearly-identified duplex feature button. (*Feature*) This allows your users to make copies on both sides of a sheet of paper. (*Function*)

"The benefit to you and your staff is *(Bridge Statement)* the ease of using just one button for your copying application. Another benefit you will enjoy is that you will save money in paper and time by copying on both sides of the paper. (*Benefits*)"

You will have to modify this formula to best fit your selling situations and the products or services you offer. However, once you begin using this formula you will be able to communicate with confidence.

Examples of Features

Once again, features are traits or characteristics of your product or service. Here are some examples.

Tangible Product	Features
Furniture	Expertly engineered, durable hardwood frame
	Natural leather cover
Felt-tip Marker	Plastic cap
	Colored-coded marker

Intangible Service	Features
Health Club Membership	Open 24-hours a day
	Personal trainers available
Life Insurance Policy	Term and Whole Life available
	Automatic insurability

Examples of Functions

Our definition of a function is the act performed by the feature. Here are some examples:

Tangible Product: Furniture

Feature: Expertly engineered, durable hardwood frame

Function: Offers a lifetime warranty on frame

Feature: Natural leather cover

Function: Gives your furniture a distinctive look

Tangible Product: Felt-tip Marker

Feature: Plastic cap

Function: The cap keeps the tip moist

Feature: Colored-coded marker

Function: Offers ease in choosing correct color

Intangible Service: Health Club Membership

Feature: Open 24 hours

Function: Allows you flexibility in your workouts

Feature: Personal trainers available

Function: Create an individualized training program

Intangible Service: Life Insurance Policy

Feature: Term and Whole Life coverage

Function: Versatility in your choices

Feature: Automatic insurability

Function: Eliminate additional physical exams

An Everyday Example

To illustrate this concept, consider the situation of selling three men a ballpoint pen. Each man has a different need for a ballpoint pen. The first man wants to save money. The second man wants ease and convenience. The third man wants to look good in his business environment. Using the ballpoint pen, we have the three elements of the feature, function, and benefit. One feature is the clip. The function of the clip is to firmly hold the pen in the man's shirt pocket. But what is the benefit? Some might say, "Well, the clip holds it in his shirt pocket, so the benefit is that he won't lose his pen." Yet, not one of the three prospects expressed the need for a pen he wouldn't lose. Our job is to **interpret the value** for these three men in order to meet their **specific needs**.

You have to convey the specific value in using your product. You can do this by using the feature, function, benefit strategy. However, you must tailor the benefits for each prospect. This example illustrates this concept.

For the first man who wants to save money, you can say, "You will like our pens. One of the features on this pen is the clip. The function of this clip is to hold the pen firmly to your shirt pocket. The benefit to you is that you will save money, because the pen won't slip out of your pocket and get lost."

For the second man who wants ease and convenience, you could say, "You will like this feature. It's the clip. It holds the pen firmly in your shirt pocket. The benefit to you is that this pen is convenient to find and is always easy to use."

For the third man who wants to look good in his business environment, you can say, "You will like the gold-enameled clip on this pen. It makes a very positive impression of quality. The benefit to you is that the pen projects the image you want to project in the business world."

In each case, you related the feature and the function to each individual's specific benefit.

Creating Bridge Statements

The purpose of the **bridge statement** is to prepare the prospect to receive the benefit. The bridge statement can be as straightforward as "The benefit to you is. . ." These are called the five magic words. "The benefit to you is. . ." These five magic words prepare the prospect to hear your benefits. Other examples of bridge statements are:

> The advantage to you is. . .
>
> You and your staff will like this because. . .
>
> What this means to you is...
>
> You'll like this because...
>
> You'll benefit because ...
>
> Mr. Jones, the *value* of our service contract is...
>
> Ms. Jones, the *advantage* of four wheel drive is...
>
> Bob, the benefits of our comprehensive coverage are ...
>
> One of the advantages our clients enjoy is ...
>
> Dr. Jones, your patients will like this because...

You should be very deliberate and precise in conveying the benefits to the prospect. Using the bridge statement allows you to monitor yourself and your sales presentations. You should practice creating several of your own bridge statements so that you can internalize using these statements.

An Example of Communicating Benefits

A dentist related a story that illustrates the value of communicating benefits and not focusing on features. This story describes the encounter of a dentist and his patient. It shows how the dentist almost missed the opportunity to communicate *real* benefits to his patient. As you can see, he corrected himself and satisfied the needs of his prospect, in this case, his 19-year-old patient.

The dentist was attending to a young lady that had just lost her two front teeth in a waterskiing accident. She was upset and still affected by the weekend incident. The dentist was a pro and he attempted to put her at ease by saying, "The repairs I will make will last you 20 years. They can also be duplicated. It will be practically painless and your appearance won't suffer." But nothing the dentist said would console her. She shook so much that he thought he would have to give her a sedative. And he did give her a sedative. Leaning down he whispered, "Even when he kisses you, he won't be able to tell." The tension went out of her body. Finally, she had heard words of real hope.

The error the dentist made the first time was in focusing on the *dental* issue and not the *mental* issue. This was not as much a dental concern as it was a romantic concern. Once she realized this, she felt better about herself and her needs were met. To a young girl the benefits were self-worth, self-value, her appearance, having dates, social acceptance, and certainly being accepted by others.

Putting the Components Together

The following is a list of tangible products and intangible services.

TANGIBLE: FELT-TIP MARKER

Feature:	Plastic Cap
Function:	Fits over the tip and keeps ink from drying out

Bridge:	The benefit to you is. . .
Benefit:	The money you save because the tip stays moist longer

Feature:	Color-coded plastic cap
Function:	Recognize the color of the pen from the cap
Bridge:	You will like this because. . .
Benefit:	The ease and convenience of finding the marker you want

HEALTH CLUB MEMBERSHIP

Feature:	Open 24 hours each day
Function:	Provides round-the-clock accessibility to members
Bridge:	What this means to you is. . .
Benefit:	Because of our convenient hours, you don't have to adjust your schedule

Feature:	Personal Trainer
Function:	Provides custom-tailored program for each member
Bridge:	You'll like this because. . .
Benefit:	You can get the best results for the time and effort you invest in your workout

Communicating Your Value

In this exercise you are to choose a product or service you sell. Choose a feature, a function of that feature, and a benefit to the prospect in using the feature. Also, include a short bridge statement to connect the feature and function to the benefit.

Product/Service: _____

Feature: _____

Function: _____

Bridge: _____

Benefit: _____

Product/Service: _____

Feature: _____

Function: _____

Bridge: _____

Benefit: _____

Success Hint:
There Are Some Guarantees in Life!

It's been said that there are no guarantees in life.

Well, I disagree. Here are some examples that dispute that saying.

Pills to be taken in threes always come out in twos. I guarantee it! The other line moves faster. I guarantee it. The best parking space is always on the other side of the street. I guarantee it. At family gatherings, my brother's stories are always funnier than mine. I guarantee it.

You see, there are some certainties in life. Here is another one: Good things happen when you work hard! I guarantee it.

As sales professionals we know this is true. The harder we work, the "luckier" we get. We also know when we slack off and engage in non-meaningful activities that our productivity declines. That is a guarantee that comes with the sales career. We know if we make one more phone call, one more drop-in visit, and ask one additional closing question that good things happen to us. Activity does drive accomplishment.

If that is a given, then what can we do to make better things happen? Good question. Here are some suggestions:

1. Make a call on that "tough" prospect. You know the one, don't you? That prospect that didn't see eye-to-eye with you the last time you called. Devise a strategy so that you will have something to say and either phone or drop by and say it!

2. Find some "dormant" accounts that haven't been called on for some time and call on them. It may surprise you that these accounts have been waiting for you to stop by!

3. Ask for referrals! How easy this is to overlook! Think about the last customer who purchased from you. Got the name? Call him/her and ask for names and contacts that could benefit from your solutions.

4. Contact your "bottom-10" prospects. You know, those prospects you think will never buy from you... Well, today give 'em a shot at you. What do you have to lose?

5. How is your "networking"? You have a network of friends, associates and business buddies who are eager to help. Make contact and let your network help you make more contacts.

Does this stuff work? The answer is: only if you do.

But I guarantee this is true: good things happen when you work hard!

CHAPTER 10:

Simply Ask for the Objective

Your Closing Attitude Versus Your Closing Skills

My friend Jay Hellwig taught me a great lesson about closing. When Jay was a top salesperson in the telecom industry, he often listened to Zig Ziglar's CDs on the "Secrets of Closing the Sale." He told me, "These are my favorite CDs on selling. Since I've listened to them, I have closed more sales."

Since there are over 50 specific closing techniques in this CD set, I asked Jay what was his favorite technique. Jay thought for a moment and said, "Oh, I don't have a favorite closing technique."

I asked, "Then how can it be your favorite sales training set?"

Jay said, "That's easy. Zig didn't teach me a closing technique as much as he taught me a closing ATTITUDE! The attitude helps me close more sales than the techniques do."

A *closing attitude*. Now, that's powerful.

Have you thought about your CLOSING ATTITUDE lately? Do you have a closing attitude? And if you do, what type of attitude is it?

Jay is right. The way you feel about closing the order is often more important than the technique you use. You probably have a number of strong closes. However, if you lack a strong closing attitude, you will never use those closing techniques.

Closing should be the logical conclusion to your selling activities. It should not be the stage of the sales process that is adversarial between the seller and the buyer. The buyer should be as eager for this stage as the seller is.

When you ask the prospect to purchase from you today, the prospect wants to know that you believe his or her decision is a solid one. You can assist with this if you have a positive closing attitude. You need to exhibit confidence during this step of the process. If you do, you will be able to expect sales success, not hope for sales success.

Jay Hellwig is right. The closing attitude will close more sales than the techniques!

The Purposes of the Simply Ask for the Objective Step

The ultimate purpose of the Simply Ask for the Objective step is to close the sale. That is, offer the prospect the best solution and agree that the prospect wants to exchange money for your solution. You noticed that the word "objective" is used instead of the word "order." Although in some situations these words are interchangeable, you are always striving to achieve your sales call objective.

There could be additional purposes to the Simply Ask for the Objective step other than asking for a purchasing decision. These objectives include:

- Introduce yourself and your company to the prospect
- Qualify the prospect
- Identify the decision-maker
- Request the opportunity to submit a proposal
- Provide a comparison of your solution versus the competitor's
- Secure another meeting
- Ask for referrals

Whatever your objectives may be, this is the step of the Sales P.R.O.C.E.S.S. where you are striving to reach those objectives.

Both you and the prospect should be eagerly awaiting this step because the prospect can solve his or her concerns and you can celebrate a sales victory.

Remember, the primary objective is to secure a favorable purchasing decision by asking the prospect to buy from you.

Why Do You Ask the Prospect to Buy from You?

You ask people to buy from you so **you can feed your family, not your ego**!

That may seem harsh. However, there is great truth in that statement. Here's why. If you are worried that hearing "no" is going to bruise your ego, you may be hesitant to ask for the objective. If that is the case, you are not putting bread on the table for your family. The reason you ask the prospect to buy from you is so he or she can solve a problem and benefit from your solution. Selling is not something you do **to** the prospect, it is something you do **with** the prospect. Through your hard work and selling efforts you are trying to improve the prospect's current situation. You should be proud to be in a profession that has that as a focus. (Selling is an honorable profession!) And when you improve someone's current situation, you are rewarded as well. Not a bad deal!

If your product is **not** going to improve the prospect's current situation, you should cease your selling activities, ask for a referral, thank him or her for the time, and leave!

Because you are reading this book you are investing in your professional growth. I would presume you are not the type of person who is going to try to force prospects to do something that is not in their best interests. The Sales P.R.O.C.E.S.S. is not intended to be implemented in that manner. This process eliminates "force fitting" a solution. Therefore, if you have gotten this far you should have a firm belief that your recommendation will benefit the prospect.

Closing is the logical conclusion to your selling efforts as you and the prospect travel through the **sales process**. By **communicating your value** to your prospect and **linking that value to his or her needs**, you have **every right to ask for the objective**.

Remember, the intent behind your technique determines your ethics. If you know your solution will benefit the prospect, then you should ask him or her to buy your solution. After all, that is the purpose of Simply Ask for the Objective.

So, the reason you should ask for the objective is to feed your family and to accomplish your personal and professional goals. Your ego will be fine. Trust me.

What Happens When the Answer is No?

When you ask for the objective and the prospect says "yes," YOU WIN!

But, what happens when you ask for the order and you don't get it? (Trust me, there will be times when the prospect says "no.")

Key point: When you ask for the objective and the prospect says "no," YOU BREAK EVEN. That's right you don't lose, YOU BREAK EVEN!

When you ask someone to buy from you, you are doing your job! No one can get upset at you if you are doing your job. Of course, you have to do your job professionally, but you are only doing your job when you ask people to purchase from you. Therefore, you break even if you ask and you hear "no." Don't take it personally.

Separate Rejection from Refusal – Revisited

Successful sales professionals understand that rejection and refusal are different. Refusal is professional. Rejection is personal. When the prospect decides not to buy from you, the prospect is declining your recommendation. That does not mean the prospect didn't accept you as a person. It does mean that the prospect has declined to accept your business offering.

For example, let's pretend you don't buy the ideas I share in this book. If you don't like my sales philosophy, I have to accept that as "business refusal." It is not personal; it is professional. As the Vice President of Sales and Training for Ziglar, Inc., I have to determine how I can improve my effectiveness so that you will buy my philosophy. That's on the professional level. Sure, it hurts when someone does not accept my sales efforts. But I have personal worth whether you accept me or not!

This is a very difficult lesson for some of us to learn. It is imperative you come to terms with it. You have invested time and energy by the time you reach the Simply Ask for the Objective step of the process. It hurts to have your work declined. We all experience this feeling. But the faster you move past this feeling, the better off you will be. The faster you accept this decision as refusal and not as rejection, the better off you will be. This is one area in the selling cycle you have to get over!

Closing Strategies

Closing sales doesn't have to be painful for you or the prospect. In fact, it's a win-win situation. Asking for the order is the natural progression of the Sales P.R.O.C.E.S.S. In most cases, if you've gotten this far, the prospect wants to say "yes" to continue the positive relationship developing between the two of you. Do it pleasantly, do it professionally, and ASK!

There are hundreds of ways to ask for the order – you've probably used several of them. Here are some closing strategies to choose from.

'Does it Fit?' Close

This strategy can be used when the prospect agrees that the solution fits his situation or overall goals.

> "Mr. Smith, do you see this fitting into your investment strategy? Then why don't we get started?"

The Comfortable Close

Sometimes the prospect expresses a need to feel comfortable when making a decision. Or, he or she expresses a need to feel this is the correct decision to make. Should you feel the prospect needs to be reassured, you may want to use:

"It appears your husband and you are comfortable with this plan. What step should we take next?"

The prospect may also comment on the importance of feeling comfortable with an organization or company that delivers customer service. You can use the Comfortable Close in this manner:

"We addressed how my company delivers on our promises. You mentioned how important this is in your decision. I believe we have provided enough information so you feel comfortable with us. Do you feel comfortable enough to place an order today?"

Sense of Urgency Close

You should use this strategy when you have demonstrated all the benefits for purchasing, yet the prospect seems a bit hesitant to make a decision. The objective of this strategy is to gain agreement that the benefit is important and there is no better time to get started than right now.

"Can you see where this would _____?" (Insert the primary benefit here)

"You are interested in _____, aren't you?" (Again, insert the primary benefit here)

"If you were ever going to start _____ (insert the benefit here), when do you think would be the best time to begin?"

Sample of the Sense of Urgency Close:

"Mr. Watts, can you see where this would <u>produce the results</u> you want?"

"You are interested in <u>receiving those results</u>, aren't you?"

"If you were ever going to start <u>receiving those results</u>, when would be the best time to start?"

One of the great benefits of these closing strategies is that you can modify the wording of the close to best fit your sales situation. You can revise the Sense of Urgency Close by asking just two questions. For example:

"Mr. Watts, you agreed our system offers better productivity. And you said productivity is important to you. Is that correct? When would be the best time to take advantage of improved productivity?"

You can also summarize the first questions and ask one question for the Sense of Urgency Close.

"We've demonstrated the savings of our productivity features and you've agreed that we can exceed your expectations in that area. Mr. Watts, when would be the best time to take advantage of these savings?"

The Simple Close

Should you have good rapport with the prospect, you can simply ask for the order. It is simple, straightforward, and the question rolls off your tongue.

"Mrs. Watts, why don't you give us a try?"

If-there-are-no-more-questions Close

You will encounter prospects who ask a lot of questions, and I mean a lot of questions. When you feel as if you have answered all the questions, yet the questions keep coming, you may want to try a tactic to wrap up the call and secure the order.

"If there are no more questions, can we schedule installation for next Friday?"

The Summary Close

This can be used when you have invested a great deal of time within the prospect's organization. You have interviewed several people. You have studied the company and how your solutions relate to the prospect's challenges. You have demonstrated the *values, advantages* and *benefits*. It is now time for you to summarize and ask for the objective, that is, to ask for a favorable decision.

"As you've seen from our presentation and our demonstration, our proposed recommendation will exceed your requirements in several areas. Your plans are to expand into three new regions this year. Our system will save you money to contribute to those expansion plans. The system will allow you to delay hiring an additional operations person until you open the new offices. In summary, our system affords you the cash flow to meet your plans. When would be the best time to schedule installation?"

The Simply Ask for the Objective step should be the logical conclusion to your selling efforts with the prospect. Don't hesitate to reach this conclusion! By doing so, you help your prospect solve problems and improve his or her present situation.

Success Hint:
Don't Quote Price Until You've Established Value

Your prospect must fully understand the value, the advantage, and the benefit of your product or service BEFORE you communicate the price. If the price is given prior to the value being established the prospect cannot relate to the return on her investment. However, if you communicate and establish your value first and then quote the price, the prospect has a chance to equate the gain she derives by acquiring your solution. She can then understand the importance to her in obtaining your product or service.

CHAPTER 11:

Managing Customer Resistance and Objections

Objections – Friend or Foe?

Objections are your friends! You should welcome objections, as they often indicate the interest level of your prospect. Some sales objections and some sales resistance are normal and desirable. Why? Because the objections indicate the prospect is evaluating your recommendation and is trying to relate it to his or her situation.

Objections can be your foe if you aren't prepared to manage them. That is, they will be troublesome if you don't have an effective methodology to confront the resistance.

An objection is defined as anything the prospect says or does that interferes with attaining your sales objective. To turn objections from foe to friend, you must possess the skill to understand and identify the prospect's concerns in a professional manner.

This chapter addresses how to gain more confidence in managing objections.

Points to Ponder About Objections

There are several traits or characteristics of objections to consider:

1. **Objections can occur anywhere in the sales process.** They don't appear just at the closing stages of the call. On my first visit to an account in my new IBM territory, the customer met me and said, "I don't like IBM right now and I'm not wild about you, pal!" This is before he'd spent 15 seconds with me!

2. **Anticipate objections and be prepared for them.** If you are selling elephants, you are going to encounter three basic objections: Where does he sleep? How much does he eat? Who cleans up after him? Use the "Law of 6" to anticipate objections. You will receive approximately 6 standard objections ... be prepared for them.

3. **Objections are either valid or invalid.** You only want to address the valid objections. Answering invalid objections will waste your time and frustrate the prospect.

4. **There are two types of valid objections: misunderstandings and disadvantages.** In overcoming misunderstandings, you must accept full responsibility for the miscommunication and clarify as quickly as possible. In overcoming disadvantages, you must outweigh the disadvantages by using specific benefits of your products and services.

5. **Prospects will make a new decision only when presented with NEW INFORMATION!** Therefore, if you make a

return call on a prospect, you should present new information. If not, you'll receive the same response.

6. **You must provide evidence in order to overcome objections.** Your challenge is to identify the proper evidence to use when overcoming various objections.

7. **There are two aspects in successfully dealing with objections: managing and overcoming.** You should first manage the objection and then overcome it! You shouldn't try to overcome it until you have managed it!

When to Answer Objections

You have several options in handling an objection.

1. Address the objection before it arises. If you know your product or service may have a feature or a function that causes concern, you can anticipate the concern and address it prior to the prospect bringing it up. For example, you are experiencing a delay in the shipping of the product. You can address the shipping delay by saying, "Once your model leaves our plant, you are assured that it has been inspected and tested by three technicians on seven functional tests. You are assured of a quality product. That is why our ship dates are three to four weeks." The strategies behind this are to address any disadvantages early, provide a reason for the delivery delay, and to assure the prospect that although he may have to wait longer, the attention to quality makes it worth the wait.

2. Address the objection at the time it is voiced by the prospect. During the demonstration, your prospect says the system looks more difficult to operate than the current

system being used. You may want to address the concern at that time. To do so, you should implement the L.C.E.T.A.A. process which is covered next.

3. Ask permission from the prospect to address the concern at a more appropriate time. In other words, if you know you are going to cover that concern later in your presentation or demonstration, you can ask, "Ms. Prospect, when we cover the investment area, we will address your concern. May I have your okay to address it then?"

If you continue to receive the same objection during your presentations, you should review the structure and flow of your presentation. This will allow you to identify why the same objection is being voiced. Perhaps **you** are causing the prospect to question an aspect of your product or service. It could result from a miscommunication on your part!

You should not be hesitant to address objections. If you are truly concerned with the prospect's well-being, then you should welcome objections. However, you must know your product, your prospect, and your sales process well enough to determine the appropriate time to confront the objection.

Managing Objections Using L.C.E.T.A.A.

You will encounter sales objections TODAY! Make no mistake about it ... you will hear some type of objection or prospect resistance today.

In order to overcome objections/resistance effectively, you must accomplish two things. First, you must understand and identify the objection before you try to overcome it. Second, you must persuade the prospect by using evidence that your recommendation has more value than does his or her objection.

Let's work on the method of identifying, understanding, and answering each objection you receive. The method is entitled L.C.E.T.A.A. We'll take a look at each of the steps in the process. Once you master this technique, you will be able to **manage** each objection you encounter.

Here is an overview:

Listen … and Listen

Clarify with Questions

Empathize

Test the Objection

Answer the Objection

Ask for Agreement

Listen … and Listen

You must listen...and listen. That is, you must listen to the **content** and to the **intent.** You must listen to the words that are being said (content) and you must listen for the meaning of the words (intent). Listen to more than the words, also listen to the meaning of the words. Is the tone a defensive one? Is the intent of the prospect to state the objection in a joking manner, or in a serious manner? Is he or she emotionally connected to the objection?

Clarify by Asking Questions

Once you have heard the objection, you should question the objection so you completely understand and identify what the prospect is really saying. You want to verify the real concern of the prospect.

You clarify by asking open-ended questions. Here are some examples:

> "What do you mean the investment is out of line with your budget?"
>
> "Why does that seem to be a concern?"
>
> "What makes the operation seem difficult?"
>
> "For what reason is a down payment an issue?"

You can also clarify by asking direct agreement questions such as:

> "So your real concern is the initial down payment?"
>
> "As I understand it, your only concern is the installation charges. Is that correct?"
>
> "Are you saying that our system won't hold up under the usage?"

This questioning strategy may require asking several questions, not just one question.

The following example illustrates using two questions to clarify what the prospect is really saying. This is a price objection where you actually ask the prospect to help you in overcoming the objection.

You have demonstrated and communicated the benefits of your solution to the prospect. You have completed the Sell Your Value step and you are now in the Simply Ask for the Objective step. You have just asked the prospect to purchase. Here is the dialogue:

> The prospect says, "We like what we see, but we are having trouble with your pricing structure."

Your response: "What seems to be your concern?"

Prospect: "We aren't used to paying that much."

You: "Help me better understand your concern. Are you saying that our solution is not worth the investment?"

Prospect: "No, we certainly see the value in your system over the one we have. We just had not budgeted that much. Now I have to get the new amount approved. I have to justify this to the committee."

By using clarifying questions you identified the objection. In the above example, it was NOT that the prospect thought your price was too high. It was a budget component that needed to be addressed. Had you not questioned the prospect to understand his point of view you may have tried to overcome a price objection that did not exist! You would have wasted your time and frustrated the prospect by addressing a concern that was not valid. There is great value in using clarifying questions.

Empathize

The purpose of the **Empathize** step is to demonstrate you care about the prospect and you are concerned with any issues that may be on his or her mind.

This is achieved in a brief sentence. It does not have to be wordy or prolonged. Simply express your concern that the prospect has an issue that must be addressed.

The shorter the sentence, the better it is. Here are some examples:

"Thanks for sharing that with me."

"I understand your point."

"I can see how you would feel that way."

The key is to empathize, not agree. If you agree with the objection, you are defeating yourself. Let's say the prospect said, "Your price is too high." If you say, "Yes, I agree," what you are saying is that you would not pay that much either. You are agreeing that the price is out of line. What you want to achieve is an understanding of why the prospect feels your price is too high. By empathizing, you can then move to the next step which is Test the Objection.

Test the Objection

In order to validate an objection, you must test it. That is, you must determine if the concern is true or false, valid or invalid. You only want to address valid objections. If you receive an invalid one, you should return to the start of the L.C.E.T.A.A. and ask a clarifying question to identify the real objection.

There are several benefits in testing the objection. By testing the objection you will discover the real reason the prospect is hesitant to buy from you. You will also discover there may be another objection in addition to the one(s) already voiced. You will save time by addressing the real issues and not false ones.

The Suppose Test

One method in testing the objection is the Suppose Test. The Suppose Test asks the question, "If that issue were not a concern, is there anything else standing in the way of proceeding?" The answer will indicate the prospect is concerned only with this issue, or there are additional concerns that must be addressed.

Examples:

> "Suppose you felt more comfortable with that issue; could we then schedule shipment?"

> "Suppose that condition didn't exist; would you then buy?"

"Suppose that were not an issue; would you then consider my recommendation?"

"Suppose that were not a concern; would we then have a basis for placing an order?"

"Suppose the amount can be justified; would you then approve this?"

The answer to the question will determine if the objection is:

A true objection

A false objection

Or, if there are additional objections.

A True Objection

For example, you ask, "Mr. Prospect, suppose you felt comfortable that the system were easy to operate; would you then place an order today?" If the answer is "yes," you know the objection was the ease or difficulty of operating the system. You now have to demonstrate the easy operation features for the prospect. By so doing, you will reach a satisfactory agreement and make the sale.

A False Objection

Once again, you ask the prospect, "Mr. Prospect, suppose you felt comfortable that the system were easy to operate; would you then place an order today?" This time the answer is "No." You would then have to ask a clarifying question such as, "Mr. Prospect, why not?" He then may answer, "Because I think your price is too high." If you know the price is <u>not</u> a concern, you may realize these are false objections. He is not expressing his true concerns to you. He may be hiding something.

If that is the case, you must confront this and ask a question such as, "Mr. Prospect, your operator has agreed our system is easier to operate than your present system. We also discussed the costs savings our 24-month plan has over the one you are using now. So there must be something I am missing. What is the real concern for your hesitation?" He may say, "Well, to tell you the truth, my real concern is the amount of downtime I'll have when we switch out the two systems." Now you have identified the true objection. It took time to get to it, but you asked enough questions to finally get to the real concern! Sometimes you have to work hard to identify the real reasons for a prospect's hesitancy.

Additional Objections

Oftentimes you will discover there are additional objections the prospect raises. Again, you ask the prospect, "Mr. Prospect, suppose you felt comfortable that the system were easy to operate. Would you then place an order today?" This time the answer is "No." You then have to ask a clarifying question: "Mr. Prospect, why do you feel that way?" His answer may indicate that there are additional concerns. You then have to ask, "In addition to the ease of operation, what other concerns do you have?" If he is being candid with you, he will then express the other objections.

The Isolate and Validate Test

There is an additional test available to you. It is called the Isolate and Validate Test. The purpose of this test is to determine if the concern is the only concern the prospect has. If it is the only concern, you then confirm and validate he will buy from you if you can successfully answer that issue. Here's an example:

"Mr. Prospect, is that the only concern you have? (Isolate the objection as being the only one.) So you are saying if you felt comfortable with that issue you would agree to my recommendation?" (Validate that he'll agree if you satisfy that issue.)

Answer the Objection

Once you secure agreement in the Test the Objection step, you can then answer the objection. You answer the objection with **evidence**. You must provide specific evidence so the prospect has confidence that you have the best solution to his problems. You must provide evidence so the prospect is satisfied you have taken care of his concerns.

The purpose of the Test the Objection step is to identify the true concern. If the objection is a true objection, it is either a **misunderstanding** or it is a **disadvantage**. You answer these differently.

Misunderstanding

If the objection is a misunderstanding, it is your responsibility to clarify the miscommunication. That's right. No matter if the misunderstanding was the prospect's fault, it is your duty to clear it up.

For example, you sell training seminars. Your contract requires a down payment for the tuition so that you can reserve a seat in the seminar. The prospect believes she needs to pay the entire tuition at the time of order. However, all you require is a percentage to reserve a place in the seminar. This is a misunderstanding and you should clarify. You should provide the evidence that you only require a percentage of the tuition with the balance paid a week before the seminar is conducted. Even though you may have mentioned this during your presentation, it is your responsibility to clarify.

Disadvantage

A disadvantage is a true fact that stands in the way of a sale. In order to manage and overcome the disadvantage, you must provide **evidence**. You must admit the disadvantage and outweigh it with *values, advantages*, and *benefits*. (You remember those three selling words, don't you?)

Again, you sell training seminars. You conduct these programs in St. Louis. Your prospect is located in Atlanta. She agrees to the value and she wants to attend. She asks when the seminar will be held in the Atlanta area. That way, she can save on transportation and hotel expenses. However, you only conduct the seminars in St. Louis. There is no misunderstanding. This is a true disadvantage. The only way to overcome this successfully is to provide **evidence** the seminar is valuable enough for the prospect to invest in the travel expenses. This may require you providing testimonials by previous participants explaining how much more productive, profitable, efficient, effective they were by applying what they learned in your training seminars. You must show evidence the additional expenses are justified.

Ask for Agreement

Once you have answered the objection you move to the Ask for Agreement step. The purpose of this step is to agree you have satisfactorily answered the objection and you can now move to the next step of the sale. Remember to use benefits in this step.

For Example:

> "Ms. Prospect, you've seen the benefits of attending our St. Louis seminar. You have also agreed the value of the course

outweighs the travel expenses. If you will provide a credit card number we can reserve a seat for you at the April program so that you can take full advantage of the training."

Providing Evidence

Objections are overcome with EVIDENCE. Not just words, but evidence.

As you relate this to your prospect, you must link the evidence to specific benefits. You may want to ask the prospect what type of evidence he or she needs in making the decision. By doing so, you can tailor your presentation to the answer.

How do you produce evidence? There are several ways to achieve this:

1. Actual percentage gains in productivity, money savings, revenue increases, and cost containment support your claims that your solutions can positively impact your prospect.

2. Industry studies and statistics may show the prospect that other companies within their industry have taken action on some of these issues. It could convince him or her that several other firms are acting on your recommendations.

3. Third party reference letters are a good method of showing proof via testimonials. This gives you credibility in a number of ways: first, the client writing the letter has experienced success using your solution; second, the client has enough confidence in you to put his or her name on the reference letter; and third, your solutions can stand up to the scrutiny of others.

4. Demonstrations allow the prospect to "see it for himself." Let him use the product. Offer him a site visit to a successful installation. Let him see for himself the process at work. There are several ways to do this, depending on the product you are selling.

Practice Providing Evidence

When communicating EVIDENCE, you should be creative. Think of ways you can prove your claims. Don't back away from providing evidence when dealing with objections.

In the space provided, list an objection you may receive and list the evidence to overcome that objection.

Objection: _____

Evidence: _____

Objection: _____

Evidence: _____

Objection: _____

Evidence: _____

Examples of L.C.E.T.A.A. in Action

The following examples illustrate how to use the L.C.E.T.A.A. when managing various objections.

Managing the Price Objection

You have demonstrated and communicated the benefits of your solution.

Prospect: "We like what we see, but we are having trouble with your pricing structure."

You: "What seems to be your concern?" (*Listen and Clarify*)

Prospect: "We aren't used to paying that much."

You: "Are you saying that our recommendation is not worth the investment?" *(Clarify)*

Prospect: "No. We see the value in your system."

You: "Then what is the hesitation?" *(Clarify)*

Prospect: "We just had not budgeted that much. Now I have to get the new amount approved. I have to justify this to the committee."

You: "I understand and thanks for sharing that. Suppose the amount can be justified? Would you then approve this proposal?" *(Empathize and Test)*

Prospect: "Why, yes, we could."

You: "Great. What does the committee need from me in order to feel this is worth the investment? In other words, what information or documentation can I present to you so that you will feel comfortable?" *(Answer)*

Notice the techniques in the above example. The salesperson used three questions in order to understand and identify the objection. Sometimes you may have to ask several questions in order to truly comprehend what the prospect means with his comment. At the Answer the Objection stage the salesperson actually asked what evidence the prospect needed in order to make a favorable decision. The salesperson should then use the prospect's criteria in supplying evidence in order to overcome the objection.

Another price objection example:

> Salesperson: Mr. Dunn, now that you've seen how my product will save you money and bring you more customers, what would keep you from signing a contract today?
>
> Prospect: You really know your product, and I thank you for your time. But based on what I've seen, I just can't make a decision right now. I need some more time to consider it and speak with our CFO to determine if there is money in the budget for this. You see, if we change vendors now, we will pay a cancellation penalty to our current vendor and I just don't want to throw money away.
>
> Salesperson: So, if your CFO says okay, you'd be ready to go with us? (*Listen and Clarify*)
>
> Prospect: No, I usually consult him, but I'm the final authority. I sign on the dotted line around here, and give him the bill.
>
> Salesperson: What kind of money are you talking about for the cancellation? (*Clarify*)
>
> Prospect: We'll lose $600 a month for the next four months if I change right now.
>
> Salesperson: Twenty-four hundred dollars is a lot of money. I don't blame you for not wanting to throw that away. (*Empathize*)
>
> Salesperson: Suppose you didn't have to lose that money? Would we have a reason then to do business? (*Test*)
>
> Prospect: Yes. But I don't like to pay twice for the same thing if I can avoid it. We have four months to go on our lease and their service really hasn't been that bad. I'm not

sure we need to go with you, but I'm also not all that loyal to them either.

Salesperson: I totally understand your thinking, and I respect you for it. *(Empathize again)* Since that's the only thing holding you back, let me show you how we can save that money for you. If you install within the next 30 days you receive a six-month rebate if you maintain the equipment yourself. *(Answer with Evidence)* I feel confident you have the resources to do that already, and I know the machine is very reliable. The maintenance will be the same routine you do for all of your other equipment. Depending on which model you choose, your rebate will be between $450 and $650 per month. If that works for you, all we need is to complete this authorization and schedule the installation. *(Ask for Agreement)*

Prospect: John, if you really could save that money for me, I'd be pleased and amazed. I know your company has a great reputation, and I believe you have been honest with me from the beginning. Let's go ahead and schedule shipment.

As you can see, the prospect was satisfied with the evidence that the salesperson supplied. The salesperson satisfactorily answered the objection and closed the sale.

Another Example

Here is the situation: You sell computer software training. You conduct classes about various software packages and are about to close an order. The prospect has 10 employees she wants to train. You must schedule these classes four weeks in advance. You can take an order by getting a 50% down payment with the balance due a week prior to the class. You have made your presentation and are now asking for the order.

> Prospect: How much is this going to cost for all 10 of my staff?
>
> Salesperson: The total tuition for this class is only $1,549.00.
>
> Prospect: Wow. That is a lot of money.
>
> Salesperson: Help me understand. What do you mean by "a lot of money"? *(Listen and Clarify)*
>
> Prospect: Well, that's a little surprising to me.
>
> Salesperson: Are you saying that this is too much for all the benefits you and your staff will receive? *(Listen and Clarify)*
>
> Prospect: Oh, no. I think it is worth the money.
>
> Salesperson: Then what is your concern about the $1,549.00? *(Listen and Clarify)*
>
> Prospect: I didn't think I had to give you the entire amount today. That's all.
>
> Salesperson: So, you want to go ahead with this training ... but your real concern is that you don't have the full amount today? Is that the issue? *(Listen and Clarify)*
>
> Prospect: That's what I'm saying.
>
> Salesperson: Well, I understand your concern. *(Empathize)*
>
> Salesperson: So, you are saying this is the only thing standing in the way of scheduling the course? *(Test by using Isolate Test)*
>
> Prospect: Yes, that's it.
>
> Salesperson: Suppose you didn't have to pay for the full tuition today, could we then schedule the class? *(Test by using the Validate Test)*

Prospect: Well, sure. We need the class. But we don't have the entire amount at this time.

Salesperson: I apologize for the misunderstanding. In my excitement to explain the benefits to you, I failed to slow down and discuss the pay plans. Our contract requires you only have to put down a percentage of the tuition. All that we require today is 50% down and the balance is due a week before the scheduled course. *(Answer by providing evidence)* Now that you feel comfortable with the payment plan, can we go ahead and schedule the class? *(Ask for Agreement)*

Prospect: Yes. Let's look at available dates.

In this instance, the objection was a misunderstanding. Once again, it doesn't matter who caused the misunderstanding, the salesperson must clarify by explaining the payment policy and options. By using the evidence of the payment plans you can overcome the objection.

One More Example

Here is the situation: You sell office copying machines. Your prospect is expanding his office and is in need of an additional copier. He has agreed to the model, the benefits, and the price. You have recommended a model that you do not keep in inventory. You have to order it from the factory. You are now in the Simply Ask for the Objective step.

Prospect: So, when can I get this installed?

Salesperson: Our current delivery time for this unit is two to three weeks.

Prospect: Oh, wait a minute. I have to wait two weeks?!?

Salesperson: Yes. That's correct. What's your concern with this time frame? *(Listen and Clarify)*

Prospect: Well, I need it sooner than that.

Salesperson: Why is that? *(Listen and Clarify)*

Prospect: We have people starting next week and we need to be ready for them.

Salesperson: I understand your situation. *(Empathize)*

Salesperson: Is that the only thing standing in the way? *(Test)*

Prospect: Yeah.

Salesperson: If you could see that the benefits are well worth the wait, would you then order today? *(Test)*

The salesperson now must acknowledge this is a disadvantage and outweigh it with *values, advantages,* or *benefits*.

One final example.

You are selling office copiers. You are in the Open a Dialogue to Uncover Needs step of the sales process. For several months your company has been undergoing much-needed changes and improvements, especially in the service department. You have gotten complaints in the past. Those problems have been eliminated and you now have statistics and surveys that prove this. You have 98% of calls responded to within the customer's expected time frame. As you are speaking with the prospect, he voices an objection about your ability to service his account.

Prospect: I have some concerns about your service department.

Salesperson: Oh, in what area? *(Listen)*

Prospect: I have heard that you guys wouldn't be able to handle our service volume in a timely manner.

Salesperson: Please tell me, what have you heard? *(Clarify)*

Prospect: Well, I was talking to an associate who indicated he had a response-time problem with your firm. Your reputation is not very stellar.

Salesperson: So your concern is our ability to deliver on our service promises to you. Is that it? *(Clarify)*

Prospect: Exactly.

Salesperson: Mr. Prospect, I appreciate your concern. *(Empathize)*

Salesperson: Suppose I can provide evidence that we have improved our service. Would you then be open to knowing more about our company? *(Test)*

In this case, the objection is a disadvantage because there have been actual service problems in the past. You must overcome this with specific evidence of improved service. You may have to provide statistics and customer surveys that prove the service problem has been corrected.

Success Hint:
Your Competition is Getting Keener all the Time... Are You?

C H A P T E R   1 2 :

The Beginning...
of Your Career

Throughout this book you have been reminded you never graduate from selling. You should always invest in yourself. School is never out for the sales professional. Therefore, by finishing this book, you are at the beginning of your sales career.

In this chapter I want to encourage you to continue to grow. A few things to keep in mind as you "grow" through your sales career are highlighted below.

Sales Slumps

It happens to all of us. It happens to novice salespeople. It happens to veteran sales representatives. Yes, it happens to all of us. What is this? Sales slumps!

All high-achieving, high-performing salespeople either just got out of a sales slump or they are about to get into a sales slump. Face reality, it is going to happen to you also.

There are two reasons you will get into a sales slump and two ways to get out of a sales slump.

1. The first reason you will get into a slump is you have lost your **basics**. You stopped doing what you knew you were supposed to do.

2. The second reason you will get into a sales slump is you have lost your **passion**. You have forgotten why you like the sales profession.

If those are the two reasons for why we get into sales slumps, then how can we get out of these slumps? How can we compress the time we spend in a sales slump? Again, there are two ways to get out of the slump.

1. Return to the basics. You should remind yourself of the activities you were doing when sales were going well. What activities were you doing that you aren't doing now? Are you using similar prospecting techniques? Similar presentation techniques? If you begin repeating those behaviors, will you realize greater sales success? Sales basics are what brought you this far; don't abandon them now.

2. Find your passion. That's right. Find your passion for the sales profession. Rekindle your passion about your career. It could come in many forms: It may be that you really are excited about serving your clients. It could be your belief in your solutions. It could be your enthusiasm about your products or services. You may remember the time you went above and beyond what the prospect was expecting. You could visit or call a satisfied client. It is suggested that you keep a mental Victory List to remind you of your past sales victories. Find a way to rekindle the excitement you have for your profession.

Hope for Success Versus Expect Success

Many years ago when I was a sales manager with the IBM Corporation, there were fourteen sales representatives on my team. As you can imagine, these reps came in all shapes, sizes, attitudes, aptitudes, and personalities. They were fun to work with and they were even more fun to observe.

I want to share my observations of two of them. At the time I worked with them, they were both rookie salespeople. Both had similar backgrounds: graduated from well-known universities, majored in business, interned with prestigious companies…they were equal in background and talent.

The difference came in their mental approach to their daily activities. One would go into his territory each day **hoping** to make a sale. The other would go into his territory each day **expecting** to make a sale. You can predict who had the best start to his sales career.

The one who had the attitude of "I hope I make a sale today" was an ambitious individual. He wanted to improve. By the fourth month on quota he realized something was wrong. To his credit, he sought coaching and instruction. He and I determined his challenge was not his skills. He knew the products. He knew how to set appointments. He could ask questions. However, his challenge was his mindset. His attitude was holding him back.

Once we identified this, he decided to feed his mind on a daily basis. He plugged in audio recordings on his way to work, on his way to appointments, and on his way home. He really did give himself a "check-up from the neck up." His last eight months of the year, he produced enough to earn himself "rookie of the year" in an office with 22 other rookies.

What changed? His mindset changed.

He began to enter his territory each day with the attitude that someone was going to purchase his products...and he wasn't going to disappoint them. He expected to sell his products. And he did.

Each day when you begin your selling activities, do you hope for sales success, or do you expect sales success?

Two Success Elements

I have been in this great sales profession for a long time. I have observed two essential elements that contribute to success, especially sales success.

The first element is this: **Develop a consistent work ethic**.

This could mean you work harder. It could mean you work smarter. Whichever you choose, you need to choose to WORK! Don't let the competition outwork you. Give it your best effort every day.

My dad and I shared a love for the game of baseball. He believed that baseball teaches a lot about life. He emphasized that you must play all nine innings of each ball game. You can't take an inning off. You can't slack off when you are in the field, you can't slack off when you are at the plate. If you do so, the other guys will get the competitive edge. You can rest after the game.

Selling is much like that. You can't take an inning (a day) off. Your competition isn't taking today off. Neither should you. You must develop a consistent work ethic.

The second element is this: **Develop a strong belief in yourself**.

You've got to believe...in yourself. Yes, as a sales professional you have to decide that each and every day you are going to hear "no" more often than other professionals. Every day you risk hearing "no." Therefore, you must develop a strong confidence in your skills, your abilities, your desire to help solve problems, your teammates, your commitment to serve, and yourself.

I am not talking about developing an attitude of conceit. What I am talking about is an inner belief telling you that you deserve sales success, that you have put forth the effort and the sacrifice necessary to reach success. You need to have a deep faith that you are capable of reaching your goals.

If you work hard, good things will happen.

If you believe you deserve success, good things will happen.

Fear Versus Faith – Choose Faith

Fear and faith have the same definition. That's right. Fear and faith have the same definition. That definition is: believing what you don't see is going to happen.

Choose FAITH!

If I can assist in any way, please contact me. I would be glad to contribute to your professional and personal growth.

Bryan Flanagan

Vice President of Sales and Training

bflanagan@ziglar.com   800-527-0306

Knock 'em Alive!

A P P E N D I X :

Sales Script to Illustrate the Steps within the Sales P.R.O.C.E.S.S.

The following is an example of an initial sales call on a prospect. The purposes of this example are to illustrate the techniques to:

- Schedule an appointment by using GBS
- Frame the sales call
- Relate using P.O.G.O. Profile questions
- Open a dialogue to uncover needs
- Use replacement selling questions
- Confirm needs
- Manage resistance and objections using L.C.E.T.A.A.
- Schedule a next appointment

(Initial call using the General Benefit Strategy)

Mr. Watts, this is James Smith with City Printing Services. We are a local provider of document imaging equipment and copier technology. I notice that your office lease is expiring on June 30 and you will be relocating to the Forrest Hill Complex. Is that correct?

Yes, it is.

We specialize in solving business problems caused by relocating offices. We've assisted other insurance companies such as yours by removing the headache of returning the older equipment while we create a seamless transition and installation of replacement equipment. The purpose of my call is to schedule a 15-minute conversation to explore the benefits you can receive with our services. When would you have a 15-minute block of time on your calendar this week?

You are with whom?

City Printing Services.

I think we are using Town Office Systems right now. I don't think we are using you guys.

Yes, sir, I understand. One of the purposes of my visit is to determine the savings and productivity increase you can receive with our systems. That's why those 15 minutes are so important. Is there a good time for you on Tuesday afternoon?

Well, let's look at 3:00. Do you know where we are located?

Yes. I will see you at 3:00. I know your time will be well-invested. Thank you.

(It is now 3:00 and you are meeting with the prospect. Plan: What is your objective for this first meeting? Do you want to RELATE? OPEN A DIALOGUE TO UNCOVER NEEDS? CONFIRM NEED?)

Mr. Watts, how are you today?

I'm okay, I'm busy.

(Frame the Call)

I will respect our time requirement this afternoon. What I would like to do is ask you a few questions about yourself, a little about your agency, some of the goals you've established, and maybe some of the obstacles you may be facing. I hope we can find some mutually beneficial areas. This will take about 15 minutes. Is that still a good time for you?

Yes. That'll work.

(Begin to RELATE by P.O.G.O. Questions)

Mr. Watts, how did you get into the insurance business?

About 15 years ago, I decided that I was not cut out to be a banker. So I looked into a few opportunities and decided insurance would be a good industry.

How long were you in the banking business?

About four years. I was moving up the ranks, but I needed a bit more freedom. My uncle suggested that I try the insurance business and it's worked out pretty well for the last 15 years.

What type of insurance do you focus on?

We are an independent agency, so we sell a full line of products. We represent a lot of the major carriers. We are concentrating on supplemental health insurance currently.

And how many salespeople do you have now?

We are up to 24. We've added seven licensed agents within the last five months. That's why we are moving over to Forrest Hill. We've outgrown this space.

That's a good problem to have. Why did you choose that part of the city?

That's a more convenient location for our guys. And to be honest, it's closer to my home.

Good for you. At City Print we sell solutions for corporate printing needs. However, I like to ask this question because it allows me to align with my client's overall strategies. So the question is, "What are your goals for the remainder of the year?"

Well, we want to get this move out of the way. It has taken up way too much of our time. At times, it has been a huge headache. That's the first thing. We need to streamline some of our systems so that we can focus on our clients. With our growth, we've taken our eye off the customer.

And once that's out of the way, what will you focus on?

Well, as I mentioned, we need to drive our business by focusing on our customers. We need to demonstrate we can out-serve the competition and we need to capture more opportunities. We are missing the chance to cross-sell some product lines.

What is keeping you from achieving this streamlined approach?

There's a combination of things. Being able to focus on it, you know, finding the time; getting the right people in place; making sure all our systems communicate to each other... those sorts of things.

(Open a Dialogue to Uncover Needs)

Yes, I understand. Thanks for bringing me up-to-date on your company and the objectives ahead of you. That gives me a better understanding. To recap, it seems that you are growing. You've added agents. You want to streamline some procedures so you can deliver on your commitments to your clients. Is that a good summary?

Yes, that's about it.

Let me ask, how does your document imaging system play into your new goals?

What do you mean?

Well, you said that you want to give better customer service and out-compete your competition. I was wondering how your system contributes to that goal.

All our systems are important to us. We use our document system to communicate; to speed things up.

What type system are you currently using?

I think it is called the Solution 2.0.

(Replacement Selling questions)

What were the features that you liked about it?

We've been satisfied with it.

What would you change about it?

I can't think of anything we'd change.

How long ago did you install this?

I guess it was about three years ago. With this move we've looked at expiration dates and I think it's coming off lease in a few months.

When you selected this system, what criteria did you use in choosing it?

I liked the productivity, it was easy to operate, and the support has been good.

As you transition to the new building, how important are those criteria to you?

What do you mean?

You mentioned the criteria as being productivity, ease of operation, and support. I was wondering if those are still important to you.

Oh, well, yes they are. Probably more important now that we're expanding.

(Confirm Needs)

Mr. Watts, if you could receive better productivity, ease and support, and maybe improve the cost efficiency, what would be the benefit to you?

Well, if you can deliver on that, we could find a lot of benefits.

And what are they?

Savings is one thing. But we need the support because we have a lot of salespeople who use the system and, as you know, they aren't the best when it comes to this kind of thing.

Yes, I can identify. Are there enough benefits to you so I could earn a head-to-head comparison on their system versus ours?

(Managing Prospect Resistance and Objections using L.C.E.T.A.A.)

Maybe. How much time will this require?

It will require very little of your time. We will run the financial comparison and present the results to you. We will research the types of usage by interviewing your key staff members. We understand how busy everyone is with the move, so your involvement will be kept to a minimum.

Well, you'll have to schedule all of that with Sharon, my office manager.

Mr. Watts, if we demonstrate how we can exceed your requirements and you feel comfortable with the system, what are our chances of doing business together?

I will tell you that we won't change for a small savings. It is too much hassle to do that.

What do you consider "small savings"?

If you can only save us a couple hundred dollars, we're not interested.

So what you are saying is that we have to exceed a set dollar amount. What amount do you have in mind?

To make it worth our time and effort, the monthly savings would have to be in the $500 a month range.

Mr. Watts, I understand. Suppose we could show you that amount of savings, is there anything that would keep us from doing business?

No, that would be it. Considering all other things are equal.

Like what?

Well, your quality has to be better, your service must be dependable, and I don't need to hear that the salespeople think it is a hassle to use.

(Confirm Needs ... again!)

So, you have to feel comfortable with the cost savings, the quality, and the ease. Is that it?

Yep. That sums it up.

I am confident we can exceed your expectations. I look forward to transferring that confidence to you. What I'd like to do is complete the research and the financial comparisons. We'll then schedule a time to demonstrate our findings and the benefits you can receive. Should I contact you directly to set that date?

Yes.

Mr. Watts, I really appreciate your time. I look forward to contributing to your company's needs in this area.

As you can see, the initial sales call was an interaction between the salesperson and the prospect. The salesperson gathered a lot of information by asking questions and listening to the answers. The salesperson succeeded in uncovering needs and confirming those needs. The salesperson is now in a position to schedule a time to sell the solution and close the sale.

WHAT IS YOUR
SALES PERSONALITY?

Have you ever noticed that not everyone behaves the way you do? There are all types of personalities that excel in selling. However, by knowing your distinct sales personality you can intentionally capitalize on your strengths and develop areas of weakness.

In less than five minutes you can learn:

- Your main sales personality trait
- Your primary approach in sales
- Your communication style in selling
- Your motivational tendencies
- Your stress areas

By identifying your specific sales personality you will learn how to sell more to more people. You will learn how to adjust your sales style to that of your prospect so that you quickly gain trust and rapport. And here's the good part — it's easy and it's FREE!

It will take you less than five minutes to answer eight questions and receive the FREE report immediately!

Simply go to www.discoveryreport.com/ziglar and find out your sales personality.